SEX *in* RECOVERY

A Meeting Between the Covers

Jennifer Matesa

Hazelden
Publishing

Hazelden Publishing
Center City, Minnesota 55012
hazelden.org/bookstore

ISBN: 978-1-61649-661-6 (print); 978-1-61649-662-3 (ebook)

Library of Congress Cataloging-in-Publication Data is on file at the
Library of Congress.

The names, details, and circumstances have been changed to protect the
privacy of those mentioned in this publication.

This publication is not intended as a substitute for the advice of health
care professionals.

Readers should be aware that websites listed in this work may have
changed or disappeared between when this work was written and when it
is read.

20 19 18 17 16   1 2 3 4 5 6

Cover design: Terri Kinne
Interior design and typesetting: Trina Christensen, Terri Kinne

❖

For those who
speak their stories out loud.

Editor's Note

The book in your hand pushes some boundaries in its quest to capture real-life situations and conversations that occur in the rooms of recovery. Some readers may find language and descriptions in this work to be sexually graphic. Hazelden Publishing's intention with this book is to show how people on the path to recovery have overcome often destructive behaviors to establish healthy, purposeful relationships free from the throes of addiction.

Author's Note

All the individuals portrayed in this book's first-person stories are real people. None are composites or inventions, and all the quotations are reported from actual conversations. But since these folks were discussing sexual behavior that usually involved more than just themselves and their own bodies, I have changed all sources' names and many of their identifying details, doing my best to protect the privacy of all involved. (More about this decision in the chapter "Privacy and Secrecy.")

Contents

Introduction

· · · · · · · · · · · · · ·

When I detoxed in 2008 from an enormous level of opioid painkillers—a level from which I'd often felt no hope of freeing myself—I noticed many changes in my body. Some changes were troublesome. For example, for many months, my body could not regulate its own temperature, and I also had difficulty sleeping. Other changes made me feel as if I'd been dead for years and had come back to life. Suddenly I could smell the flowers in my garden. I could appreciate the flavorful nuances in meals. I could hear the harmonies of music in psychedelically beautiful ways. And all of a sudden, I wanted sex.

Several years before my detox, as I was bombarding my migraines and fibromyalgia with massive doses of opioids, and during my subsequent loss of control over the drugs that were supposed to be helping me function, I had become disturbed by the waning of my sexual response. When my desire returned so suddenly and strongly in detox, it was almost as disturbing as having lost it during active addiction. I felt out of control, I felt intimate contact was unfamiliar without any substances to "manage" it, and in many ways I felt I did not understand what sex was for.

When I traveled the country to talk with clinicians and recovering people about my book *The Recovering Body: Physical and Spiritual Fitness for Living Clean and Sober*, I discussed how I had learned about my sexual response, initially using a vibrator. Almost all the questions I took from audiences were about sexuality. One that I will never forget came from a therapist at a women's treatment facility, who approached me after the Q&A session because she was shy about posing a question

1

about sex in front of a large audience. "We don't let the women have vibra-tors," she said, "and we tell them they can't have relationships for the first year. So how can we help them get in touch with their sexuality?"

I was chagrined that I didn't know how to respond to this question. There I was, standing on a stage, celebrating how well the body could re-cover in so many ways from the devastation of addiction—and yet there was a whole swathe of women who, it seemed, were barred from learn-ing about their sober sexuality in the simple ways I'd learned about mine. And to add a lock to the bar on the door, it's a fact that we don't talk about this stuff in recovery circles. By "this stuff," I mean sex. By "recovery circles," I mean the whole gamut: from Twelve Step recovery to harm reduction and everything in between.

On the one hand, with a continuing epidemic of heroin and opioid painkiller abuse, addiction and recovery remain in the public spotlight. As I write this, President Barack Obama has requested $1.1 billion from Congress to fund the Comprehensive Addiction and Recovery Act, which would funnel money to states for programs that offer Suboxone mainte-nance among other treatment strategies.

At the same time, on the other hand, the public is also confronting questions of sexuality, especially marriage equality and the difficulties faced by transgender people. Again, as I write this, Bruce Springsteen just made headlines by canceling his concert in North Carolina because of its infamous transgender "bathroom law." Two recent books about sexuality—one by a sex educator, Emily Nagoski's *Come as You Are,* and one by a journalist, Peggy Orenstein's *Girls and Sex*—have touched a deep cultural nerve by investigating women's persistent lack of knowl-edge about their own sexual pleasure. Yet few of us have explored how addiction, recovery, and sexuality are related—indeed, intertwined—often from early childhood on.

Just think: Why do so many people start using drugs and alcohol in their teen years, just as they start exploring their sexuality? Why do so many people in recovery have histories of trauma—not just physical abuse, but sexual; not just sexual trauma, but *childhood* sexual trauma? As the therapist who challenged me with her question that day was suggesting: If substance abuse and addiction distort our perceptions of pleasure, what would it mean for us to recover normal, healthy perceptions? Why are fellowships that practice Twelve Step recovery so apparently bent on denying newcomers—both women and men—the capacity to explore their sexual pleasure?

When I left the gathering that day, I was determined to work on answering these questions. I wasn't sure what I'd find out, but first I looked for other books that might have explored this subject. The most recent one I could find had been published almost twenty-five years ago—a slim literary volume long out of print. Clearly, this was a topic in need of fresh discussion. Right off the bat, its author made the excellent point that when we detox, our bodies wake up. My working title for this book was *The Awakening*, after Kate Chopin's 1899 novel about a woman whose body wakes up and leads her to make seriously countercultural decisions. After my own experience of waking up, I set out to collect the stories of people in recovery from substance addictions. I would hear them give their "sexual leads," to use a well-known phrase: *what it—sex—was like before, what happened,* and *what it's like now.* This book does not deal with sex addiction. Many books out there do, but none explores sexuality in ordinary recovery.

I interviewed thirty-five people in recovery from addiction to alcohol and other drugs. They were women and men ranging in age from twenty-four to sixty-seven. They identified as straight, gay, gender-queer, gender-fluid, and transgender. They were Asian, black, Latino, white, and multiracial. They lived on the East Coast and the West Coast, and in places in between. What they all had in common was that they had passed some time in recovery without drugs. I talked with people who were married, single, and in more- or less-complicated relationships, and I didn't focus on marital status as much as I did on the ways people brought recovery principles to bear on their sexuality. We didn't talk about "how to date in recovery." There are articles and podcasts galore about sober dating. Instead, this book digs into questions and problems that real recovering people have when they start taking their clothes off—without drinking or using substances in order to do it.

In conversations ranging from one to three hours, the interviewees eagerly talked about their sexual experiences. Often they left saying that telling their stories had been personally meaningful; some had discussed events and feelings they had never even admitted to their partners. On one or two occasions, they shared experiences they'd never shared with anyone. I asked more people for interviews than I had time to speak with, expecting that some would decline. And yet no one turned me down. In the course of those interviews, it became clear to me that we in recovery want to talk about sex and sexuality, but we don't know how to open the discussion. I opened it for them.

This book is designed to continue that discussion. Between the covers of this book, I've convened a special meeting to help us begin to talk about sex. What I've done here is booked the space, invited a variety of speakers to share their experiences, and brought up an array of topics that might help all of us begin to investigate our own experience—and eventually, like the speakers in this book, to tell our experience out loud so we can see it, discuss it with trusted people, and move beyond it.

In the first section of the Big Book of Alcoholics Anonymous, in the original 164 pages, I counted 578 words about sex.[1] Since that particular book is the earliest and still one of the most widely read, deeply scrutinized, and influential pieces of recovery literature, some of these words are legendary. Everyone I spoke with, whether they attended AA or not, knew that "some people would have no flavor for their fare, while others want a straight pepper diet." These euphemisms for the range of sexual experience in recovery, while perhaps helpful in approaching a dialogue about sex in 1939, the year the Big Book was published, simply don't cut it today, when we're facing a hookup culture fueled by apps, alcohol, and an epidemic of prescription opioid and heroin addiction that, ironically, kills sexual response for the many who live with it.

A chorus of voices is now calling for more medications to reduce cravings, specifically in the form of buprenorphine preparations such as Suboxone and the new implant Probuphine. These advocates have been concerned primarily with preventing overdoses and the spread of HIV and hepatitis C through injection use. What they seem to be unaware of, or ignoring, is the way opioid-replacement medications can affect sexual response, especially in the high doses at which they're prescribed in the United States. In more than six years of covering addiction issues in my blog and in the press, I have heard from many people across the country (and indeed the world) whose sex drives have been depressed—some say crushed—by huge doses of maintenance drugs. This is a serious detriment for the quality of human life, and it can lead to clinical depression, among other disorders. Yet few researchers, policy makers, or clinicians are talking about the problem of sexual dysfunction on opioids or opioid-replacement medication.

We're seeing something similar to what happened in 1987 when the Food and Drug Administration approved fluoxetine (known by the trade names Prozac and Sarafem, among others) for the treatment of depression. The manufacturer claimed that sexual dysfunction was a rare side effect, but it's now known that the vast majority of those who take Prozac experience anorgasmia, erectile dysfunction, lowered libido, and other suppressive sexual side effects. Few studies have explored the sexual side effects of methadone and buprenorphine; most have limitations and almost all have studied only males. We need more extensive and reliable research on the side effects of these anti-craving drugs, especially among women, to weigh their possible long-term negative impact on users' health and quality of life along with the good they might do in preventing overdose and relapse.

It is hard to get funding to research projects connecting sexuality and addiction that does not explore sex addiction per se. Scientists at major research universities told me repeatedly that quite simply no research exists about the effects of substance abuse and addiction on sexuality, and that it's difficult to secure institutional approval—let alone money—for anything regarding these two hot-button issues. But while this book is not meant to be a comprehensive, analytical work of journalism, I wanted to offer some scientific context for the personal experiences included here, and so I spoke with some professionals who could give readers that helpful frame of reference. They include, for example, Nina Jablonski, professor of anthropology at Penn State and a world-renowned researcher of the evolution of human skin; Tiffany Field, a psychologist who directs the Touch Research Institute at the University of Miami School of Medicine and perhaps the foremost researcher of human touch; and the revolutionary Emily Nagoski, self-proclaimed "sex nerd" and author of the aforementioned book *Come as You Are: The Surprising New Science That Will Transform Your Sex Life*. Nagoski's revelation that "pleasure is not addictive" was particularly helpful (and a relief to know!). She told me, "The pleasure of your own skin, of your organic body? Not addictive. But people can use sex as a way to escape. They can use it as a strategy to cope with loneliness or anxiety. When they get into this cycle of using sex in that way, it's not the same thing as experiencing pleasure." So as recovering people we need to learn how to distinguish pleasure from escape. That's one of this book's goals. And it's one of the keys to overcoming addiction that nobody talks about.

Nagoski also declared that we simply do not know the connection between sexual response and addiction, *because nobody has studied it.* Why should we study it? Because every member of the tribe of *Homo sapiens* needs connection, including sexual connection, and addiction is notorious for breaking down human connection.

While interviewing the participants for this book, I discovered that many, if not most, people with addiction have sexual trauma, which is why it emerged as such a prominent theme in these pages.

Many of the people I talked to across the country were not just physically abused, but also sexually abused—some as adults, and many as children. I did not choose people to speak with because they had this issue; rather, as I spoke with person after person, out it came:

My uncle had sex with me from the time I was eight until I turned thirteen.

My stepfather used to take my clothes off and put his hands on my genitals. I think my mother knew.

My neighbor, after school, would force me into his basement and make me go down on him.

This wasn't true for everybody, but the frequency was in line with the statistics you'll learn in the course of this book. They suggest that at any given meetup of recovering people anywhere, many of the people around you have experienced sexual abuse. I wanted to share these stories and talk honestly about difficult topics such as abuse and trauma in this book because as a society we do not talk to each other, or our children, in any kind of sane, practical way about sexuality, and we lack the language to ask for help when we most need it, especially in traumatic situations.

So this book is a repository of some of the most tender, intimate, and often explicitly (and painfully) honest witnessing that one human being can hear from another—a gift from some courageous people who down to the last one expressed a hope of helping others explore their sexuality inside recovery. As I heard common questions and themes in these stories, I began to imagine myself as the chair of a special meeting—a "meeting between the covers"—where people could speak openly about their experiences, and where I, as the chair, could bring up topics.

The structure chosen for this book reflects that meeting approach. Half of the chapters in this book are true personal stories, told by recovering people in their own words. Alternating with these are "topic chapters," my own reflections on some recurrent themes that are central to sexuality, addiction, and redefining our sexual selves in recovery. These topics were brought up repeatedly by both recovering people and experts. In addition to trauma, these subjects include:

- the infamous "One-Year Rule" on sexual abstinence in early recovery
- the concept of virginity and the various meanings and implications that charged term carries
- the difficulties we experience in making ourselves vulnerable by being honest about our sexuality
- the roles pleasure and touch play in sexual connection
- the differences between privacy and secrecy
- the physical and emotional consequences of our damaging sexual behaviors, both in addiction and in recovery, including the much-discussed "Thirteenth Step"
- the essential act of making amends to the people we've harmed sexually, including ourselves

Each of these topics is followed by "queries" designed to help support discussion with partners, friends, therapists, sponsors—and within ourselves. (More on these queries in a moment.)

The book ends with the stories of three people, all in long-term recovery, who have grown—partly through inquiry into their own sexuality—into a greater sense of agency and self-actualization. While the details of their accounts are different, the stories themselves impart similar messages. Tom tells us about discovering honest sexuality in the face of a progressive disability; Olivia describes finding her way after growing up in a sex-positive environment; Gabriel reflects on self-acceptance—however challenging that might be. Told here without follow-up topics or queries, their stories offer examples of recovery strengthened through sexuality, and bring our meeting to a close in a powerful and considerate way. With stories spoken very much out loud.

This book is not about defining how to do sex "right" or "wrong" in recovery. Nor do I offer explicit solutions to particular sexual problems. Recovery is a highly individual process, driven by the particulars of each person's unique physiology and psychology, and when you add sexuality into the mix, the "solutions" to problems are even more varied. For example, readers in detox who find my blog often email me to ask the question that's impossible to answer: "When will I feel better?" I can imagine readers detoxing from heroin or painkillers writing to ask, "When will I stop having spontaneous orgasms?" or "How long will it take until I can actually feel someone touching my bits again?" It can take a few weeks to regain normal sexual response—or, as one researcher mentions later in this book, it can take months or even longer. Even then, many factors can play into it: for example, self-stimulation versus stimulation from others. In other words, a guy might be able to get off quickly by himself, but he might not be able even to feel his partner touching his penis until his body and mind fully recover.

With all those variables, anyone who says they can tell us how long it will take is deceiving us.

In recovery, no one can give us the fail-safe. Instead, what we're doing here is gathering an assortment of experiences and principles that can, when considered deeply, help most of us discern what's best for us sexually at whatever moment in recovery we happen to be inhabiting.

A lot of us who read self-help books think that if some genius would just give us the answers to a few simple problems—when to tell your date that you don't drink; how to meet people when you no longer go to bars; how to answer the question "Do you drink?" in a dating profile; how to have a hookup without using; and so on—with those answers, we'd solve this big dilemma and we'd be waking up next to the partner of our dreams. But think about it: these questions have roots that stretch back into our histories. For example, if we've spent decades drinking or using to take our clothes off, to manipulate our sexual response, or to numb the degradation we may have experienced early in life when someone violated us—when we get sober, these problems are way more complex than "how to date." They come from unresolved experiences that have led to feelings of unworthiness and fear of finding out who we are.

Which means that the underlying purpose of recovery, and of sex in recovery, is to find out who we are.

And who can tell us who we are? Who can figure out for us how to let go of the unworthiness? It's not a matter of reading a manual, answering questionnaires, looking for the right TED talk, or even "figuring it out." Like other problems in recovery, it's a matter of patient, solo inquiry. That's what the queries in this book are for. You'll find them at the end of each of the "topic" chapters. Queries are a powerful spiritual discipline I learned in twenty years of participating in Quaker community. They're "open-ended questions that guide reflection on ways our lives and actions are shaped by truth and love. The emphasis is on how to live a life more completely aligned with the life of the spirit." They're meant to be returned to again and again, with the idea that, as we continue to open our minds to the questions, more will be revealed.[2]

These may not be easy questions to consider or to answer. But for real: how would another person be able to solve the problems in *your* sexual history? Even the best therapists can't do that.

But we can do it ourselves! If we make a continuing study of it.

While working on this project, as I've mentioned to people that my next book is about sex in recovery, I was frequently asked, "What did you find out?" Maybe the most important thing I've learned is that sober sexuality in adulthood would come more easily if we could talk frankly and directly to kids and people in general about sexuality. Let me say this in words of mostly one syllable: we need to talk to our kids about sex. People usually ask, "How? My sixteen-year-old refuses to discuss the subject." But the discussion doesn't start at sixteen. It doesn't even start at six. It starts in the "terrible twos," when kids first begin to ask questions.

Like many kids, my son was close to three when he started asking where he had come from. And like most American moms, who grew up with minimal sex education (some of which was truly hair-raising), I didn't have ready answers for these questions. Hell, I've never felt like I know what I'm doing as a mom! I've made up most of my parenting on the fly. I framed my answers in terms he could understand—"You lived in a place right behind my belly button, you came through a tunnel in my body, and I was so happy that day." Our openness about sexuality has continued to the present. Partly because of these open dialogues, and coupled with the fact that he's an athlete who takes care of his body, my son—unlike myself—has grown up with no hatred for or fear of his own body. He accepts the human capacity for healthy pleasure.

So he hasn't wanted to get drunk or stoned to have relationships with girls.

You might ask, "How do you know he doesn't drink or use?"

Because he has told me. Because he rightly claims his privacy, but he displays a nature that's pretty much devoid of hiding—deceit being a hallmark of drug abuse.

Because he has earned my trust. And I've earned his.

This book is about growing a vocabulary to help us talk with each other. It's about helping us explore who we are sexually, and what we want. For as hard as it can be in our society to talk about either addiction or sexuality—and how much harder to talk about both at once!—one lesson we learn in recovery is that difficulties can be eased by gathering our community around us and accepting their help. I hope this book helps us all find language to say out loud the sexual experiences it might help us so much to talk about.

. . .

Ready to tell your story out loud?
Talk about your
#SoberSex experiences
with Jennifer Matesa on
Twitter @Guinevere64
and on Facebook
@JenniferMatesaAuthor

AMY

Running Around the Apples

Twenty-seven / One year in recovery

I was really young—I wasn't even five. And my uncle, who had been in prison for killing his wife, he . . . well, the aftereffects have been pretty catastrophic for me. But the actual event itself? I mean, yeah, even though I was only four, I can remember the exact way the room looked when he took me in there with him.

I've remembered it off and on throughout my life. But it took quitting drugs and alcohol for me to be able to start talking about it to anyone. I mean, anyone. I was probably six months clean and sober before I could say anything about it. I remember I was riding my bike, and it hit me—this *happened*. Not only what he did, but the ripples of that in my life. I was just bawling.

That was the first time I had felt anything about it. I was twenty-six, and for more than twenty years I had never let myself feel anything about what had happened.

I drank for the first time when I was twelve. So I used alcohol and then drugs for more than half my life to try to keep from feeling the feelings. Plus I had an eating disorder, which began at the same time I started drinking and which was completely related to my disconnection with my body and my sexuality—my refusal to feel anything.

Then around fourteen, I started smoking weed. We lived in New Jersey; my dad was a tree farmer for a long time, and he also just happened to grow pot, right? So by the time I was sixteen, I was going to school and waiting tables and I had a car, and I was getting high every day. One day my mom found my bowl in my car. This was her way of dealing with her daughter's smoking weed while driving: She wrote me a note, *Can you roll joints, please?* That was my parents' idea of teaching me to be responsible. I guess they thought that, for legal purposes, joints would be better than a bowl! You know—I could throw the joint out the window more easily. Or something. If it were up to me, and I had a kid, I would take the bowl from their car. And then I would really want to have a conversation, like, "Don't drive while you're high, okay? It's a bad idea!" Maybe take their car keys? Today it would definitely lead to a talk.

In college I smoked weed every day, I drank a lot, and I did a lot of Vicodin. I paid for the weed and alcohol, but I didn't pay for the pills. My friend's mom had cancer and she wouldn't take them, so I had an unlimited supply. They were the ten-milligram extra-strength ones, and I'd take two or three, and always when I was drinking.

In college I worked thirty hours a week, but I couldn't figure out why I never seemed to have any money.

About six months into recovery, I went to a Twelve Step yoga meeting with a friend of mine in the program. Somebody brought up the topic of resentments toward men who had hurt or sexually abused women. Sometimes men come to this yoga meeting, but that day only women were there. During the meeting I didn't open my mouth about what had happened to me. I just listened to all these other women talk about their experiences. I hadn't known so many other women had had the same kind of thing happen to them.

And then during the meeting my friend spoke up and said she had *also* been sexually molested when she was a child—which I hadn't known. I don't know how she brought herself to talk about it, because she was super young.

So then, after that meeting, I told my sponsor.

And after I started talking with my sponsor, what my uncle had done to me and my feelings about it finally became accessible to me with language. I started to be able to talk about it. I started to go there in my mind. I could think about the fact that, yes, he had stuck the muzzle of a gun inside my vagina when I was only four years old, and there was nothing I could do about it.

Being in a room with women who were vulnerable, and especially with women who I think were also edging toward forgiveness rather than just being blind with anger—that was helpful to me. Because I didn't want to hold on to this anymore. I was six months clean and sober, and in order to heal I wanted to start letting the bad shit go.

I started understanding that maybe what he had done and my refusal to talk or even feel about it had made me quiet in my life. That was my part in it—refusing to feel or talk about it. I'd been quiet about asking for what I wanted in sex. Quiet because I felt I had this man's shame. My uncle's shame—I felt I'd taken it *into* myself and my body. I definitely think that might be one of the reasons it happens to so many girls and women—to take away women's ownership of their bodies. And it can be a very effective means for men to unload shame and anger onto women.

Recovery has given me the ability to begin to take back ownership of my body.

Talking with my sponsor about it was a big part of being able to feel again too. Coincidentally, when I first talked with my sponsor about it, I was doing my Fourth Step.

Before we formally did the Fifth Step, I was meeting with her weekly. I don't even remember how the fact of the abuse came up. I think we were just talking about relationships, because I had started dating someone, and she was like, "I want you to really think about what you're doing sexually during this first year." She didn't tell me I couldn't date for the first year. Even if she had, I wouldn't have listened, right? I mean, come on!

And I think she knew that. She said, "You've listened to everything I've told you so far. Why is my caution about sex the one thing that you're willing to ignore?" And I was like, "Because I'm twenty-six!" At this age, that's a long time to stay away from sex!

She was like, "Okay! Just be careful."

I think her biggest concern was my own sense of self. Whenever I was dating someone, she'd continually ask me, "Are you losing yourself? Are you still doing the things you need to do for yourself and your spiritual growth?" She didn't want a relationship or a sexual experience to replace my spiritual growth. And I think I did need to hear that.

This last year—this first year in recovery—has been the first time in my entire life that I've ever had sober sex. It's just so scary. It's sooo scary! I mean, for real: I was afraid to be without my socks on in front of another person. I was horrified! I felt, just, *so incapable.*

Do you know how people say that if you were high when you studied for a test, you should be high when you take it? Like there's a room in your mind that's marked "High" where all the shit you did while you were high goes, and a room that's marked "Sober" where all the shit you did while you were sober goes? . . . People actually say that. And sex was like that. I just felt like those two things—sex and drugs—had always coincided. There was no part of my brain or body that had *only* had sex.

But eventually, having sex without drugs became okay. I think in general sex is important, but I also find it to be one of the more playful aspects of life. And I think my playfulness about it helps me not to take it so seriously. It helps me not feel victimized—as if sex is something that's done to me.

Sober sex has also become okay because for the first time I'm not trying to give myself away to somebody. I'm trying to be there with this person, and to do this thing that feels good with them, but I'm not trying to unburden myself on another person.

One way I used to have sex was just to conquer someone else. I had pleasure, but not all the time. I've had between thirty and forty sexual partners—I wrote every name I could remember in my Fourth Step inventory—and while writing it all out, it became very clear to me that what I wanted was not pleasure, it was validation. Out of all those thirty to forty people, I had orgasms with only two. I got off on the conquest, the way I could lock eyes with someone else over the bar and know they'd be going home with me. I liked being able to feel I could *get* this person. Validation was like winning, and the sex itself was not even secondary, it was like superfluous. It wasn't even the point. The point was that I could use another person to find validation for myself.

So then I found out when I did my Fifth Step with my sponsor that this way of doing sex was totally selfish and self-seeking.

I also used to have sex just to give myself away. When I was dating people for longer amounts of time—like for more than six months, maybe even a couple of years—I definitely thought of sex as the only way to prove there was intimacy in our relationship, whether I really liked the person or not. Before I got sober, I would either pick people up to conquer them, or I would convince myself to stay in longer relationships that I didn't belong in.

Now those behaviors are no longer options for me. I can't just use someone, and I can't stay somewhere where I would lose myself or be required to give myself away, because then I would use or drink. Now I have to be honest. And yeah, one way I'm honest is, I pay attention to my body.

I'm not so good with commitment, is the thing. I've been working on not doing the fade-away in people's lives. That's what I do—I date for three months, and then I ghost, and I just don't speak to them.

Would you believe that in sobriety I've found out that's not a good way to treat people? Including myself.

Or else I cheat on them. But I haven't cheated on anyone since I got clean.

I've been working on having conversations with people about not wanting to be with them, or what's wrong in the relationship. It's self-centered fear: I ghost because I'm afraid of them not liking me; but the fact is, I don't really like them anymore. Or else I've become afraid of dealing with their emotions. That happened with the first guy I dated in sobriety. Awesome guy, very handsome, very smart, and super intense. After a couple months, I was like, "Okay, I need some space." I think it was mutual. We were seeing each other maybe two or three times a week.

So we had this little conversation about needing space, and the next day we ran into each other at Whole Foods, and guess what—I was running around the apples, trying not to talk to him.

I even said to him, "I'm trying to find the right apple!" Right?

In my head I'm telling myself, *You don't want to deal with this—you're fucking running away from him!*

The thing is, that's what I used to do before, when I was using. I'd run around the apples, trying to hide. And that didn't even feel like fear! It just felt like a reasonable solution to a problem: you run! But in sobriety, I was like, "This is bad! I'm running around the apples! This isn't normal."

I had to do an inventory. I had to look at why I was avoiding honest conversations. I started to think about why, first of all, conversations I could feel in the air with my parents just never happened. We never talked about my being molested, about their drug use and drinking—those kinds of conversations. The way I was taught to get through problems and feelings was just to ignore them, and drink or use.

And learning the right ways to deal with problems in sobriety hasn't fixed me immediately. It's still at times excruciatingly uncomfortable to be inside my body. My humanity is insufferable to me.

But trying to be honest and self-aware has made discussion so much easier.

I think we're so afraid of our bodies in this culture. And we're afraid of the truths about our bodies. I think we're taught not to say a lot about our bodies in our relationships. It's all up in our heads. And it's hard to remedy that, because it's really damaging—this lack of honesty about sex and our relationships. I think the hardest thing, and why it's important to talk more openly about sex, is that it can't get better unless we're willing to speak about it. And that's hard because no one's really talking about it.

So there's very little language. With regard to sex specifically, there's sexually exploitative language—the language of porn, the male-centered kind of porn. But there's still a big silence about sexuality as it relates to honesty and intimacy. So I'm trying to create that language for myself. And it's bit by bit, and two-steps-forward-one-step-back, right? Because obviously, in recovery, one day I do my Fifth Step and take a big leap forward, and the next day I see myself: *Oh my god, here I am, running around the apples.*

The Infamous One-Year Rule

. . . .

Any of us who've been going to a Twelve Step fellowship to stay away from alcohol or other drugs knows what I'm talking about when I bring up the One-Year Rule.

Practically every newcomer hears a version of the One-Year Rule. It pisses everyone off, and almost nobody follows it.

Because, *whaaat???*

No Sex for One Year?

This is what single people in my region hear: "No sex for a year."

In other regions, I found out, newcomers might hear, "No new relationships or marital changes for a year."

"This prohibition on sex for one year is a real disincentive for young people to get sober," said a twenty-six-year-old man with eighteen months of sobriety who'd been told not to have sex for a year. "If you finally make it that far and you hear from your sponsor or in some meeting that you can't have sex for a year—so forget about dating for a year—it's like, why even try to get clean?" He came to understand that suggestions like the One-Year Rule are not absolute and shouldn't be taken as ironclad. "Otherwise," he said, "there are so many things that would have turned me away from recovery."

Still other regions or meetings, surprisingly enough, might swing in the opposite direction by telling newcomers, "Go have as much *sex* as you want, just don't try to get into a relationship."

"When I first started going to meetings, I was told you can't get drunk with a dick in your mouth," a forty-something gay man from New Orleans told me, a man with twenty years of continuous sobriety. I asked him what he thought that colorful recommendation meant.

He said: "What that means is, oh god, yes—have all the sex you want! When they say we practice these principles in all our affairs, they do mean sexual affairs as well. We don't stop any part of our life till we get to Step Twelve, so why would we stop having sex? But—and this is a big 'but'—as you learn the principles of recovery, you have to incorporate them into your sex life. I've never heard of a prohibition on sex, but the suggestion to hold off on new relationships is a really good one."

Why It Might Be a Good Idea

Often, when we're instructed not to make any big changes in the first year—not to start a new relationship, not to end a long-term relationship, and maybe, if you're single, not even to have sex with anyone but yourself in the first year—it's the first time we have to think seriously about surrendering our ideas of what we want.

Because sex is something most of us want. And to give it up for *a year?*

Oh yeah and by the way: There's *nothing at all* to that effect in any recovery program's recorded literature, or in the *Diagnostic and Statistical Manual* (which is "How It Works" for shrinks). All these "suggestions" are part of a vast lore that has grown up among people in long-term recovery from addiction for the past eighty years or so. For most of that time, we recovering people have had to take care of our own encounters with addiction mostly by ourselves, because the scientists and the medical and psychological practitioners, which is to say the professionals who might help us, haven't yet known enough or achieved enough unity to develop effective strategies against this thing that's out to kill us—be it a spiritual malady, a bio-psycho-social illness, a brain disease, a genetic or epigenetic disorder, a learning disability, a Cyclops- or Grendel-like monster, or whatever you might call it.

As fellows in the project of recovery, we bond and support one another through the age-old means of story—which casts both the newcomer and the old-timer in a web of belonging and safety. Community.

And one story that's been passed down among our many recovering tribes is this: it's just better not to make big relationship changes in the first year. Whether you're single or in a relationship, it's good to think really hard about what sex means to you, how you used to use it, and how you might want to engage with it differently as you start having it sober. All that takes time.

In early recovery we're vulnerable physically and emotionally—we're craving the relief of the head-changing stuff we've just overcome—and the excitement of new sexual relationships can tempt us with instant relief and satisfaction that quite literally activates the same chemicals—dopamine, endorphins, adrenaline—as the drugs we've just quit using. Homer inscribed it this way into *The Odyssey*, an ancient epic poem of a great journey that for centuries was passed down orally before it was ever inked onto papyrus: our boats have steered clear of the temptations of the Sirens, our bodies have just been cut down from the mainmasts where they'd been tied for safety, and to turn the wheel toward anything that even sounded like the Sirens' song would be a super-bad idea. It could hurt others, and it could hurt us.

But guess what? Being human, most of us do it anyway.

Making Recovery a Top Priority

The One-Year Rule is related to another cardinal recovery suggestion: make your "program" the first priority in your life.

Which sounds well and good. But it can be unnerving to drag one's newly detoxed body to church-basement meetings and drink shitty low-end coffee out of a Styrofoam cup, wishing you could jump out of your skin, listening to people with years of recovery tell you you'll lose anything you put in front of your "program"—including whatever new romance might actually be the only promise of relief from early recovery's soul-crushing grief of never again being able to take another shot, drink, pill, or toke.

So when it comes to sex, most people ignore this cardinal piece of advice. It's like the one legal thing left, right? Not one person I talked to—young, old, male, female, straight or fluid, this-that-or-the-other race—had followed the rule just because they were told to do it by some-one who had "more time" than they did.

"Everybody's going to tell you not to get involved in your first year," said Gabriel, who tells a story later in this book about kicking addiction in New York City thirty years ago. "And out of the thousands of people I've known in recovery, I've known of only maybe five who have actually ad-hered to that. So go ahead and get involved, but understand that you're going into any involvement probably for the wrong motives, because no-body in early sobriety does stuff for the right motives—or maybe only a handful do. Just understand these things: it will likely end, because you are not a formed person, and it will likely expose you to certain risks, es-pecially of intense feeling that you or the other person may not be able to handle. The only way to protect yourself against that risk is by making your program your top priority."

So: do what you feel, maybe, but check your motives with yourself and with other people you trust. If you haven't done your Fourth and Fifth Steps yet, including looking at your "sex relations" while you were drink-ing or using, you may want to do that before you hop between the covers with somebody new. The Big Book (p. 69) gives some useful guidance, both in looking at past relationships and in thinking about getting in-volved with someone new:

> We reviewed our own conduct over the years past. Where had we been selfish, dishonest, or inconsiderate? Whom had we hurt? Did we unjustifiably arouse jealousy, suspicion, or bitterness? Where were we at fault, what should we have done instead? We got this down on paper and looked at it.
>
> In this way we tried to shape a sane and sound ideal for our future sex life. We subjected each relation to this test—was it self-ish or not?

Still, a lot of people flout the rule and even tell their sponsors so. A lot of sponsors I've talked with have at some point thrown up their hands at these decisions, as if they were parents: *Kids these days—what can you do?* Sometimes sponsors and even whole local recovery groups draw hard lines of intolerance over first-year dating. One young woman who got sober in New York told me about a meeting that had revoked the home-group membership of someone who broke the One-Year Rule.

Sponsors are people too. And groups are made up of people, and people make mistakes.

Gabriel himself started a new relationship within the first three months of quitting drugs in 1986. Still, he committed to making his recovery the top priority in his life. That meant he never skipped meetings to be with his new partner, who he'd met in a recovery meeting. "It's not the best idea to date somebody in recovery, but where else was I going to meet somebody? I wasn't consciously setting out to do that, but meetings were where I met new people, and there were a lot of hot women there," he said.

When Sex Stops Working as a Drug

As with any other topic for discussion in this book or in meetings, stories about the One-Year Rule are countless. We all have to find our own way through the dark forest of early recovery, evading the Big Bad Wolf and working hard to build our houses with bricks instead of straw. (It takes a lot more time and energy to build with bricks, by the way.) But listening to a lot of people's "sexual leads," as I did, some commonalities emerge. For example, when we start having fully conscious sex for the first time, many of us wake up in the morning with the realization that the person who took off our clothes the night before cannot do for us what we can't do for ourselves. Sex partners can't be God or higher powers or god-things because it's not helpful to surrender our wills and lives to another individual in any way, including through sex.

"Sex stopped working, and that was the main reason my attitude around it had to shift. Like any drug, it stopped working and it started hurting," says Adrian, twenty-eight, who has seven years of recovery. "I mean I was crazy about some girls, and pretty obsessive. And sex wouldn't give me what I needed, and eventually I realized *they* couldn't give me what I needed. Cause they weren't a higher power—it wasn't their job to give me relief from myself and my own mind. I was asking too much of them."

So with nine months in recovery, and with no suggestion from anyone else, Adrian decided she wanted to take some time off. She told her sponsor that she'd take a year away from any kind of sexual interaction with anyone but herself. "My sponsor was like, 'Yeah, I think it's a good idea.' So I was celibate for nine months." She pauses. "I mean, let's be real, I jacked off like a crazy person! But yeah—no kissing, no touching, no cuddling. *Nine months!* I wanted to go a year, but hey."

The Sirens seemed to be everywhere, tempting her to break her promise to herself. "People knew I was doing this," she said, "and they came out of the woodwork. It's like they smell it on you and decide they're gonna go after you. It's hot to try to seduce somebody who has decided to be celibate! I met some really cool people and I wanted to have sex, but I told myself, 'No, I'm not doing that.' I had these crazy crushes and daydreams—I just didn't act on them."

Adrian decided to end her sexual abstinence at nine months because she realized she wanted to date a woman who, in her words, "I really liked, and she liked me, and we had been friends for a while." So it wasn't a matter of using someone sexually for escape.

"I'd learned what I needed to learn," Adrian says. "I learned to care more about other people. I tried to right-size the importance of sex in my life. I had a better relationship with my spiritual practice at that point."

· · ·

Queries for Discussion

The Infamous One-Year Rule

☐ When I think about taking a break from sex for a certain period of time, what are my first responses? What are some responses that underlie the initial ones? Human beings are born with an intuitive capacity that we lose in addiction and begin to regain in recovery. What does my intuition tell me I need to do?

☐ Whether I'm inside a relationship or not, how long might I be willing to consider taking a break from sex? If I'm not willing, why not? If I am willing, how much time do I think might help strengthen my recovery?

☐ If sex were taking priority over my recovery, how would I recognize it? What would that look like, and how might I respond? What practices might I put into place to safeguard against this risk?

☐ Have I subjected a new potential sexual relationship to the Big Book's test: "was it selfish or not?" What do "selfish" sexual conduct and motives look like to me?

DON

Doing the Dishes

Sixty-seven / Forty years in recovery

I was a couple of years younger than my classmates, and for that reason I became sexually active earlier. I started having sex around fourteen, and the girls I was having sex with were about two years older than I was. The year before that, I had started doing drugs—mostly weed, and also some psychedelics.

The sex I had was almost entirely outside of caring relationships. As I got older, often I was in a sexless romantic relationship and, outside that, having sex with other people. Maybe it was because it was the sixties, and maybe not, but that situation persisted until the second half of my first year of college.

I became attached to a particular woman, but I felt the peculiar dilemma of not wanting to be faithful to her but also not wanting her to have sex with anyone else. This is strange to talk about because I've never really talked about it with anyone, but any sexual relationship I was in, I had little or no consideration for the other person, either sexually or really in any other way.

When I was a junior in college, I was arrested for something I didn't do. The cops let me go, but the whole experience made me think carefully, and I decided I'd stop doing drugs. In fact I didn't stop doing drugs, but I kept them out of the house. That was the rationale: using wasn't bad, it was getting arrested that was bad. If I was at a party and there were drugs, or if I needed methedrine for "scholarly purposes," it was acceptable.

At the same time, I also decided I was going to get married. I figured the tension I always felt between wanting the comfort of a steady relationship and not wanting to be monogamous—that tension would magically go away if I just got married. That was what young men of the time were supposed to do—settle down and get married! I was nineteen. She was nineteen. It didn't work out. I like the phrase in one of the stories in the Big Book—"an extended one-night stand." We lived together for maybe two years, and it took her another year to get around to divorcing me.

Nothing changed, especially from a sexual point of view. I didn't have that many opportunities during my marriage to sleep with other women, but when I did, I gladly did it. And I had no real concern for those women's wants and needs, sexually or any other way. I lied. I'd always cheated on women. I'd have sex with them and never contact them again. I had no interest in their sexual pleasure.

I didn't graduate from college, but I stayed in town and became a bartender. After my wife and I separated, I was rarely without a live-in companion. But there came a point when I was living alone. When that happened, I told myself that one of the reasons I spent all my time in bars must be that I was looking for female companionship. One night, I decided to instead just go out to have a nice time—I'd put on some really nice clothes and go to this nightclub, just to hear music. No sooner does the music start than this woman sits down next to me. I knew her—I'd been very attracted to her years before, but she had dismissed my attentions because she had a kid. She said, "Look, Don, I have this kid to raise. I need to be responsible." I thought to myself, *What bullshit is that? She's out of her mind!* Which just shows you how little empathy I had for women.

So that night she sits next to me just as the music's starting, looks over at me, and says without any introduction, "Do you want to fuck?" And truth be told, I *didn't!* I wanted to listen to the music. But, you know, you can't *say* that. The definition of being a guy is you're always looking for it, always ready for it. My nice night turned into a disaster. I no longer had any illusions about why I spent my time in bars.

At this point in my life, I'd been arrested many, many times. I'd usually brawl with police. I blacked out regularly. I thought it was normal. Well, it is, if you're an alcoholic. Eventually, I became unemployable, ran out of money, and moved back in with my parents on Long Island.

Finally I went to see a psychiatrist in the city, a guy who actually knew about alcoholism. He recognized my problem and referred me to an alcohol specialist, and that led to rehab. I went to Chit Chat Farms, which is now the Caron Foundation, but this was back in the time when rehabs were "drunk farms." After I detoxed and finished rehab, they recommended I go to a halfway house in New Jersey.

From the time that woman in the nightclub propositioned me until the time I went to rehab—two years—I had no sex. It wasn't difficult, given how much I was drinking and using. In rehab, though, I began thinking about sex a lot.

One day early in my stay at the halfway house, I said I had to go back to Long Island and spend the night there, using some fictional reason. Actually, I was going to spend the night with an old girlfriend. I went to her house, and she made dinner. After dinner, I started to wash the dishes. And she freaked out at me, screaming at me, asking what the hell's the matter with me. My doing the dishes was too out of character. So I went back to Jersey. I turned down a night in her arms. I realized I didn't want to be around people who had the old expectations of me.

When I was in college I'd had a friend who had mental illness, and he spent a lot of time in the psych ward. The times he was out, we hung out together, but the problem was he was really crazy, and I guess I wasn't—I was just a dope fiend and a drunk. When I got married at nineteen, he decided he'd get married too. He married a lovely young woman from the college I'd gone to. And after I got divorced, he also got divorced—it didn't work out for him either.

So at a year sober I was still living in the halfway house, and one day I was back on Long Island visiting my parents. And I knew that my friend's exwife was living on Long Island too. She and I had kept in touch, and when she found out I was visiting, she invited me over. Somehow I knew it was more than just an ordinary visit between friends. I remember driving over to her place and thinking, "Oh my god, why am I doing this? She's my friend's ex-wife. If he finds out you're thinking about sleeping with his ex-wife, he'll go nuts."

And this is interesting—I had slept with the wives of many friends, but never the wife of that particular guy. I just never, ever looked at her sexually. I said to myself, "What are you doing? This is crazy. If you do this, you'll end up drinking." I felt so many layers of forbiddenness about getting together with her.

But then on the other hand I thought, "Why not? What's the problem?" I wasn't in a situation where I could call my sponsor from Philadelphia. There were no cell phones back then. Long-distance calls were very expensive. There was nobody I could talk to about this, so I actually prayed about it. I hadn't been in the habit of praying, but after praying, I became calm and decided, "Why not go see her? You don't know what's going to happen. Don't worry about it."

So I went to see her. And we did have sex pretty promptly. We kind of began a long-distance relationship.

I moved back to Long Island not because of her, but because I'd accidentally found a job there. So she and I ended up in the same city. I had my place, she had her place, but in a year we moved in together. About two years after that we got married.

I was just kind of trusting I would know how to handle properly whatever came up. That's the intuitive ability that the Big Book talks about: "We will intuitively know how to handle situations that used to baffle us."

She was my first relationship after I got sober. It's hard to say how sex was different after getting sober. For one thing, we did talk about sex, and I don't ever recall doing that with any other woman. We asked each other, "What do you like?" or "How was that?" and "Could it be better?" Even these questions would have been unthinkable before.

Men just didn't talk that way then. For example, while I was living in the halfway house, I was reading a book by Art Buchwald about a bunch of prominent people describing their first time having sex. Their stories were all the same: "It was terrible!" I remember my roommate asking what I was reading. I told him, and I asked what his first time having sex was like. He said, "Ask me that again, and you're gonna get my fist in your mouth." Which probably would have been my own reaction to a question like that, even from an intimate partner. Maybe not so aggressive, but I would have shut down the discussion just as firmly.

I think practicing rigorous honesty helped me have these conversations. But more than that, it was like washing dishes. When I first got to the halfway house and saw that I'd been assigned to wash the dishes, I thought, "Oh my god, how degrading." And what's worse: "I don't know how to do that!" But it felt so good when I actually did it. I think that was my first intimation that I could be a somewhat normal, fulfilled person without drinking. That was really a lesson in living with other people and being considerate of their needs.

That's what talking with my wife about our sexual experience was too. It was simply being considerate and curious about another person, rather than just seeing what I could get out of the encounter.

I have been tempted to cheat inside my marriage. I've been aware of opportunities, and I've declined to get further involved. And then I'm sure there are other opportunities that I haven't been aware of, simply because I don't go there in my mind. I saw that behavior on my part as a character shortcoming that I asked to be removed. And since I've been married, I haven't been propositioned like I was by that young lady in the nightclub.

I'm a big fan of the Big Book's words on sex. It basically says that as long as you're not putting yourself first, as long as you're not being selfish, whatever you do is okay. Your main consideration is the other person or people involved.

I've told the men I work with in recovery: You really need to look at your motives. Are you just doing this out of selfish desire, with no regard about how it may affect the other person? When we do things we regret, that's not healthy for our recovery. If we do something selfish in recovery, we do regret it. That's the kind of thing that keeps you up at night and works at you. Regrets are an analogue to resentments. We all have them, and part of the project of recovery is minimizing those, especially the big ones, and often the big ones are about sex.

Virginity

. . . .

I can't believe our society still uses the word "virginity." Think about how much moral judgment is loaded inside the barrel of that word. And it's aimed especially at girls and women. After all, from the time we're children, what do we learn that being a virgin means?

The term "losing your virginity" actually accounts for a very narrow window of sexuality. Most people think it means putting Tab A into Slot B, when the tab is a penis and the slot is a vagina. This ignores the sexuality of gays, lesbians, transgender people, and people who identify as fluid. But even for straight-up heteros, there is so much more to sex and sexuality than just tabs and slots.

Why talk about virginity in a meeting about sexuality and recovery?

Stress

Because the idea of virginity causes us more stress than we may think. And although stress doesn't cause addiction or relapse, there's a strong correlation. Stress that we don't know how to negotiate creates a big risk for addiction for those prone to it, especially if we aren't given, or don't pick up, the tools to negotiate it.

It's important to talk about virginity in a recovery meeting because inherent in the idea of virginity are the experiences of loss and deprivation. When we value virginity above honest inquiry into our sexuality, we have to think about when to lose it, how to lose it, with whom to lose it, whether we're ready to lose it. Protecting it. "Saving" it. "Pledging" it—giving it to some person-as-yet-unknown. So then our sexuality becomes about loss: imagining losing it, actually losing it, remembering how we lost it.

And the sense of loss doesn't disappear after so many acts of inserting Tab A into Slot B. In other words, you can't get rid of the residue of loss just by having lots of sex. When we grow up thinking sexuality is about loss, the loss stays with us after we have sex. It lives inside us. And a chronic feeling of loss is essentially a wound that won't heal.

As human animals, our birthright is a natural desire to have sex. But virginity, if you'll excuse my French, fucks that all up. When we haven't yet had sex but we're getting ready to, we hope we're going to do something that feels awesome and that connects us with someone else—but the idea of "losing our virginity" means we're about to lose something unique and invaluable forever. So in buying into the ideas that we've inherited about virginity, we put ourselves between a rock and a hard place.

Perfect place to drink or use.

Dirt and Division

The idea of virginity, as defined by most of Western culture, makes our sexuality dirty.

For millennia, especially for girls, virginity has been associated with moral purity and personal value.

"I had sex at fourteen because virginity was a heavy cross to bear and I just wanted to get rid of it," says Patty Powers, a sober coach who travels the country helping people stay on their games in recovery. "I didn't like how sex divided people—between those who *did* and those who *didn't*."

The word "virginity" is part and parcel of the reason I don't use the word "clean" when I talk about my recovery. I don't mind what words other people use to describe their own experience, but I rarely say I'm "clean," and I would have a hard time seeing the word "clean" encoded in addiction and drug policy. As a little Catholic girl, I was taught that as long as I stayed a virgin I'd be "clean"—so, tacitly, I learned that girls who "lose" or "give away" their virginity are "dirty." In the same way, the culture teaches us a label for what those of us in addiction prove we are by dropping random urines that show we've been using on the sly: *dirty*.

I believe everyone possesses basic goodness that makes us "clean" at our cores. No matter how many drugs we've used, no matter how much or what kind of sex we've had, and no matter whether we're inside or on the other side of active addiction, we are clean at heart. Inside addiction, we may not feel connected to that cleanness. Recovery teaches us how to connect.

Brutality

It's important to talk about virginity in recovery circles because the word encourages people to split hairs, to think in terms of "technical virginity." This is especially true for young people who may not have much language for their sexual experiences and who may have no reliable sources of information about sex.

A forty-year-old woman named Ava, for example, told me she had loved her college boyfriend and wanted to "lose her virginity" with him. But she didn't trust the intuition that told her she wanted to connect with this guy in that way, so she drank to relax during any sexual contact. Because drinking and using encouraged her to numb and abandon herself, she became more and more separated from her sexual desires and expression. Eventually, as she entered her twenties, her virginity became a burden. She broke up with the nice guy and went and picked a brutal, heavy-drinking older man to "get rid of" her virginity.

And once he realized he had a virgin on his hands, she said, he was more than delighted to do the deed.

"I was raised serious hardcore Catholic," Ava said. "My first boyfriend after college was this very heavy-drinking CEO—a very emotionally closed-off guy. I was twenty-two; he was thirty-five. We'd had three or four dates. One night I'm sure we'd had a few drinks at dinner and then polished off a six-pack together back at my apartment. We were making out, and he took my skirt off, and when he tried to stick it in, he realized I was a virgin. And that *really* turned him on. 'Are you a virgin?' he asked me. I told him I was. And within the next minute, he was ramming me right there on the rug. It was lucky I was drunk, because it hurt, like, *a lot*. I had saved my virginity for so long, and when I finally made the decision to lose it, it was very, very painful."

The act itself was consensual, but afterward, she said, "I felt like he'd reamed me out with a hoe handle." She said she bled for three days, and she drank to get rid of the ugly feeling she'd been left with.

"The guy was pretty brutal," she said. "And I just thought, 'Well, that's what sex is. It's gonna hurt. Like a lot of other things in life, it's going to hurt. And if you want to have that closeness, you're going to have to accept that pain."

So we have terms for "losing your virginity" like "busting" or "popping your cherry." The names themselves become punishing self-fulfilling prophecies, not to mention prominent cultural images that depict women in pain during sex.

Deceit and Distortion of the Truth

Oral sex has become super popular among high-schoolers and college kids because they can have sex without thinking of themselves as "having sex." So it's workaround, a deceit. And deceit—distortion of the truth—is a sentinel feature of addiction. We addicts lie, and even though we often deny it, the lie hurts, so we drink or use some more to get rid of the pain of supporting the lie.

Those of us who have grown up in addictive families learn we have to obey the rules to keep the peace, and usually one cardinal rule is: *Never put Tab A into Slot B*. If we abide by this rule—or if we don't but lie to our families and say we have—just to keep the peace, we give away ownership of our sexuality to an addictive family system. But deep down, inside our bodies, we know we're lying, and to live with the pain of lying, we drink and use. Coincidentally, that's another thing we learn from our addictive families: that drinking or using is a solution to problems.

And the older we get, the harder these habits are to break, and the more difficult it becomes to uncover and clear up these deceits. We just keep letting other people own us.

Losing Your Virginity

Because we get used to thinking about all the sexual contact that is not "intercourse" as "not really sex," we tend to discount all the sexual experi-

ences we've had with real people early in our lives. It compartmental-
izes those real sexual experiences away from the defining moment of
"losing our virginity," which marks the moment—so say our parents, so
says society—that we're Actually Having Sex.

Hayden, who tells her story in the next chapter, told me, "'Losing your
virginity' is such a stupid term."

"If we get rid of that term, what marked your sexual initiation?" I
asked Hayden.

"In that childhood type of way, it was when I was exploring with my
childhood best friend," Hayden said. "We were twelve. There was no penetration. There was touching, groping, kissing, all of those things, but in a
twelve-year-old sort of way, with another twelve-year-old girl. I had never
seen anything sexual before that, so I had no idea."

This was an innocent exploration between two kids entering puberty,
an age when many of us are taught we should never talk or even think
about these experiences, because they're "bad." Their innocent exploration didn't fit with the conventional ways society defines sex because it
was between two girls, with no "Tab A into Slot B," or, as Hayden says,
"there was no penetration." So Hayden came to think of this experience as
"not real sex," even though it made her feel good and connected her with
someone about whom she cared deeply.

She compartmentalized this experience away from what she thought
of as her sexual life.

"After that," Hayden said, "I shut off any sexuality." Until, that is, she
was in her late teens, when she met her first boyfriend, with whom she
had "real sex"—tabs and slots—but who was controlling and abusive. And
she cheated on him and on every subsequent partner she had, until she
chose recovery.

Sexuality Is a Continuum, Not an Event

Healthy sexuality can be seen as a continuum of intimate self-expres-
sion and communication with others. It has less to do with "busting your
cherry" than fostering human connection.

In recovery, we can begin to imagine sexuality differently. What if,
instead of being a threatening experience—one that "deflowers" us, that

robs us of the beauty of our innocence—our first sexual experiences might create *more* beauty in ourselves and our partners?

If we take these pressures off sexuality and begin to think and talk about it more honestly and directly among ourselves and with our children, then we can remove some of the fear and shame that leads us to abuse drugs. We can simply do what our bodies are made to do: connect sexually in healthy, non-destructive ways.

• • •

Queries for Discussion

Virginity

☐ Make a list of the first times you used alcohol or other drugs in connection with your sexuality. Go back to the first time you had any sexual contact with anyone, even if you weren't drinking or using regularly at that time. What did the substance do for you that you could not do for yourself?

☐ Who would you be if you thought of yourself and your body as fundamentally good, worthy, clean, and beautiful? If you thought of yourself in those ways, what would you do—and not do—sexually?

☐ What would your life look like if you truly owned your sexuality?

HAYDEN

Forgiveness Can Heal

Twenty-eight / Three years in recovery

Starting with my first boyfriend, Drew, until I got sober, I cheated on everybody I dated. And none of them knew this. I hid it. I had such intense fear. I felt like, if I didn't run away from someone, they would do the same thing to me that Drew did. Or what happened to me when I was eleven might happen all over again. So I couldn't let myself be honest with anyone.

Instead of being honest, I would just go have sex with someone else.

My mom was always extremely sexually provocative. Like to the absolute *extreme.* Raunchy. Vulgar. Like when she's at the bar, she'll get up on the bar and start stripping. And as a kid, it totally mortified me. But at the same time, I had sexual desires. And I always felt like, "I don't want to be like my mom."

But I'm *soooo* like my mom.

So I didn't know how to have my sexual power without being disgusting.

Still, I can see how my mom derived a lot of power from her raunchiness. And, in an awesome way, she never inflicted any body shaming on me. She's always been pretty overweight, but in a very feminine way. Voluptuous. And also very powerful. She's maybe an inch or two taller than me and very strong, big-boned—just a lot of physical and sexual force to her. As an adult, laying her own addiction aside, there's something I admire about that force. But I also feel like she uses that raunchiness instead of developing other kinds of power—productive skills, and emotional health and well-being.

I developed sexually super early. I got my period when I was nine and still in elementary school. That was mortifying to me. And when I started getting attention from guys, like from older men—which is totally gross, because I was seriously only ten years old—I guess that's when I started to become really ashamed of my sexuality. And some people say we don't live in a rape culture! It absolutely threatened me, the way these old guys would talk to me and leer at me.

When I was eleven, I was molested in some way so that I woke up the next morning in pain. It happened at home. I don't know for absolute sure what happened, but I've always had a suspicion about who did it. One of my mom's best friends from when she was a teenager, he saw me grow up. Like I said, I developed really early, and I was very stereotypically pretty. This guy would be either extremely lewd with me and make a lot of comments about my body, or he would treat me like a little kid and roll me around on the floor—too much touching.

In fact, when I was about twenty-one he found me on some social media site, and he tried to message me a couple times. I didn't answer. He sent me this really long message. When I first opened it, I could see there was a lot of sexual stuff in it. The beginning sentences were the start of a sexual scene. I had the guy I was dating at the time read it for me. He said, "Don't ever read that—it won't be good for you."

When I was twelve, my childhood best friend and I both started to explore sexuality with each other. Even though it was innocent, that experimentation was also something that was shameful too, because I grew up in a poor town in the mountains, and in retrospect I can tell who some of the queer kids were, but back then everyone had to present as "straight." So when that girl the following year came out as bisexual, it was like a big scandal.

Drew was my first boyfriend. We dated for two years, starting when I was sixteen and he was twenty. What attracted me to him was that he cut himself, and I had started cutting after I was molested. That was my very first addictive behavior. I cut until I was maybe twenty-one.

So next thing you know, Drew and I are buddies, then we're making out, then having sex—it was all very quick. But he was somebody with a lot of problems of his own. Even just looking at him, he was covered with deep, big-time scars that he had inflicted on himself. He had a lot of anger.

Within four months he had moved into my house, and he became physically, emotionally, and sexually controlling. I didn't understand how super controlling he was until more than a year in. I mean, I was sixteen! And my parents had let him move in! And every time I told him I wanted out, he'd threaten to kill himself.

It was a crazy thing to be a teenager and have this baby-man—a grown man with no emotional intelligence at all—controlling everything.

And my drinking was daily from the start, at sixteen. My parents knew about it. My mom would always say, "If you're gonna get drunk and fall off the porch, I want it to be my porch."

The first time Drew and I had sex, I didn't really want to. We had no conversation about it. I was so afraid and clenched up—probably due to what had happened in my childhood. There were several nights when he tried to have sex with me and he couldn't penetrate because I was so physically closed up.

So he was like, "Let's drink!" And we drank and drank, and eventually I was drunk enough that it happened. It was a really quick thing. And that was the first time I had sex.

I didn't use a condom, and I wasn't on birth control—I wasn't on it for a couple months—but we always had unprotected sex. He's the only guy I've ever had unprotected sex with. So having sex with him started the fears of getting pregnant, getting diseases. Actually *having* sex added layers of fear to the *idea* of having sex. So of course there was no pleasure to it.

At this point my parents were into their own addictions. By the time I was sixteen, everybody I was close to was smoking crack. This included my parents, Drew, most of his friends, and even my childhood best friend. I thought I was so strong and clean and *not* an addict, because I wasn't doing crack.

Meanwhile, I was getting shitfaced every day.

I finally ditched Drew by joining the military in the middle of my senior year of high school. Joining the military was totally ridiculous because I'm a pacifist and an anarchist. So I'm like, "Let's go to work for the government, in the business of war!" What a solution. Yet it was my way to escape. I lived in a poor town, and they gave the military entrance exam to the entire class, and I scored really high. So there were recruiters looking for me all the time. One day a recruiter basically locked me in a room—I spent the *entire day* in a room with this guy—and he was like, "You want to go to college, right? How are you gonna pay for college?"

And in my mind I was like, *I dunno—everybody around me is smoking crack. What do you suggest?* But I told him, "I guess so." And he promised me I'd never get shipped overseas. It was maybe three years after 9/11. So I joined the National Guard. I thought to myself, I'm gonna get away from Drew. Every one of my shots at breaking up with him had been met with suicide attempts and insanity.

In fact, when I finally broke up with him for good, he overdosed on a bunch of pills in my bed. I didn't go to school that morning because he was convulsing. He turned blue and I called 911, and the paramedics and some cops showed up.

And I remember the cop who worked in my school also showed up, and he actually asked me why I wasn't in school. And I was like, "Are you kidding me? There's somebody dying in my bed right now! Like, what the fuck are you saying to me?"

So if I'm telling my story here of "what happened" in terms of sexuality and addiction, I can say that by this time my sexual history was marked by a very early sexual assault and then this abusive two-year relationship that filled my whole mind with so much pain. But I'd also had this wonderful, beautiful experience with my childhood best friend that I'd always chalked up to youthful exploration—but at least it was like, we loved each other, and it wasn't screwed up, and I wasn't assaulted in the locker room by a boy. Because I know people who were.

Also, from the time I was fourteen, I was in and out of psych wards. If someone names a list of psych meds, I was on most of them, and they gave me at least three diagnoses. And on top of all the psych meds, I was drinking alcoholically, which I always lied about—that is, until I was twenty-five.

That's when I actually got into recovery: I was going into a psych ward again, and for the first time ever I told the truth about how much I was drinking. I had called a crisis network and said I wanted to kill myself. The nurse who was doing the intake for the crisis center asked very sweetly, "Do you think *drinking* might be your problem?" Well, by this point I was finishing a handle of tequila every day or two. And, like, a handle is *half a gallon.* The name comes from those little handles that are always on those big bottles. So I was drinking a ton.

I have no idea how I decided not to lie to that nurse. That was a god-moment. Lying came so naturally to me. I'd always told people I drank maybe two drinks a week. I never *thought* about lying—the lies just tumbled out of my mouth. So I don't know why the truth came out that time. I was hallucinating, and when I told the nurse it had been a day and a half since I'd had a drink, she told me I was going through withdrawal.

So I detoxed through the psych ward and they wanted me to go to sixty days of inpatient rehab, and I said, "Noooo way! That is *not* happening."

They sent me off with a meeting schedule, and the first meeting I went to was at 6:00 on a Friday evening. Everybody looked so nice; they had all just come from work, they were all in their nice clothes, and I thought to myself, *There's nobody queer here.* Then I said to myself, *Hell no.*

The next day I went to an LGBT meeting, and I still thought the same thing, because even though there were lesbians there, they were all super old.

Every meeting I went to, I looked around and thought, *Oh my god, are you kidding me? There's nobody here like me.*

Until I met Amber. I didn't meet her at a meeting, but she saved my life, man, with her tattoos and metal and combat boots and her super-intense brand of honesty. We got sober side by side. We have the same sponsor. I first saw her at a friend's rooftop party. She wasn't sober yet, but she was like, "Yeah, I go to meetings sometimes." I clung to her as the only person I found who was like me. It planted the seed that maybe someone like me could find a place in recovery.

In adulthood, before I got sober, I had started dating women, and I developed this idea that women were perfect. The first one I dated was an active heroin addict, and I thought she was just *amazing!* Classic bad decision—one addict getting involved with another. I was twenty-two.

At the time I'd called the crisis hotline and got help, I'd been dating another woman. She was living in my house, and I'd kicked her out with no notice, just "Get the hell out!" Unbelievably nasty. Later, I saw her again during my Ninth Step and told her I knew how wrong my behavior was. Then I started to get some peace of mind.

I could not find that peace of mind until I eventually took the Steps. Like I said, I'd already been on all kinds of psych meds and other drugs, but they never got me there. In rehab, they offered me Naltrexone and stuff to stop my cravings, and that might have worked, but I refused to take it. If people decide to take that stuff, it's okay with me, but for me, it wouldn't have touched my deep desperation. And that's the problem I've had since I was a kid, since before I was cutting or using anything—this big desperation inside me. That pit of darkness and despair that caves in on itself.

Being without drugs and alcohol in early recovery and being suicidal—in that super-sick frame of mind, "one day at a time" was not the solution for me. I was grasping at sobriety day after day. I said to myself, "If this is all there is, I'm *out.* I'm gonna kill myself."

What I was refusing to try was anything having to do with spirituality.

That was never an option for me before, and here was my sponsor, telling me that it was the only solution. We spent like eight weeks on the First Step, meeting every week, reading out of the Big Book. I'd started asking myself what it would be like if I stayed the same, knowing there was no way I was going to last because I was so close to committing suicide by that point. It felt like my sponsor was telling me that spirituality was the only thing left to try, and it ticked me off to no end.

I guess I started trying to take the Steps almost to prove her wrong. I thought it wouldn't work for me because I was too far gone. And I just thought it was stupid.

I didn't feel the spiritual awakening or any of that until I started my Ninth Step, and the first person I made amends to was the woman I'd been sleeping with who I'd kicked out of my house. And she actually forgave me.

I haven't made amends to the really big people in my life yet. Like I haven't made amends to my mother—I haven't even seen my mother since I got into recovery three years ago, and I'm not clear yet what kind of harms I might have done her. But I can now see that if I keep staying clean and sober, if I keep living on a spiritual basis, all that will become clear.

I just look at that woman's willingness to forgive me for my kicking her out of my house and throwing her stuff on the street. Her willingness to forgive me—when people ask me now, "When did you first feel the presence of God?" I tell them it was in that moment.

Trauma and Shame

....

In her 2015 memoir *Blackout: Remembering the Things I Drank to Forget*, Sarah Hepola writes about some of the sex she had during alcohol blackouts. In fact, she opens her memoir with a dramatic story from her twenties: having blackout sex in a Paris hotel, then waking up from the blackout naked and locked out of her room. She had already been drinking for at least ten years. And the beginning of her drinking life coincided with the first time she had intercourse. She met an eighteen-year-old guy, and they had a one-night stand. She was just thirteen.

After she got sober, her best friend gave her a tape recording of Hepola herself telling the story of that first sexual encounter shortly after it had occurred. Almost forty years old when she listened to this tape, Hepola writes that the experience of a one-night stand at thirteen with a young man of eighteen "explained a lot about my mixed-up history with drinking, men, and sex." The guy lost his erection several times, and Hepola writes that "he never went that deep in." She gave him a hand job and a blow job and, at just thirteen—we girls learn early, don't we?—she pretended she liked it. This passage appears near the end of a two-hundred-thirty-page book.

"I think you can make the argument that I was much more damaged than I acknowledged," Hepola told me. "Nobody gets a printout that says, 'This is what happened to you, and here are the effects.' I know that when I was thirteen, fourteen, or fifteen I liked to look at that experience and re-write it: 'I was in control and I'm awesome and cool.' When I was eighteen, nineteen, or twenty, it was: 'I think I was assaulted.' It just kept changing."

Hepola felt shame, confusion, and fear after this experience, and like many women who've had similar experiences, she was trying to control the pain of her feelings by telling herself different stories about what had happened to her. But the stories didn't make her feel better. So—again, like many women—she drank.

After *Blackout* was published, most interviewers ignored this graphic recollection of her first sexual encounter. They were more interested in how she got locked out of her Paris hotel room naked. In the book, Hepola does not label what she experienced at thirteen as rape, and she said she thinks this made some interviewers reluctant to bring up the subject of that encounter. But we talked about how important it is in recovery to discuss the intricacies of our sexual experience so we can better understand them. "There's an opportunity to talk about the complexity here," she said. "What is sexual trauma?"

Some Facts about Trauma and Recovery

For many of us, trauma happened early in life—before anything else related to our addictions. And then, sometimes, drinking or using led to even more trauma.

This is a fact: While we're sitting in any given recovery meeting, the majority of those around us have experienced some kind of trauma, including childhood sexual trauma, and it's not restricted to women. The research is clear about the connection between childhood sexual trauma and drug and alcohol abuse. A 2012 study (Huang et al.) of 196 alcoholics in treatment found that one-third reported childhood physical abuse and one-quarter reported childhood sexual abuse. The authors called for improved assessment of alcoholics in treatment with respect to childhood trauma, and for "an early focus on parenting skills that attempts to minimize children's exposure to different forms of trauma" in order to reduce psychiatric problems and early reliance on alcohol to negotiate stress.[3] Stephanie S. Covington, PhD, who oversaw some of the first research on women, addiction, and trauma, reported that three-quarters of addicted women have experienced sexual abuse and half have experienced physical abuse.[4]

Covington's research does not focus specifically on childhood abuse, but the landmark Adverse Childhood Experiences (ACE) Study does.

The ACE Study, which included more than seventeen thousand partici-pants, identified ten early traumas, including sexual traumas, that result in physical and emotional problems later in life. Compared with kids who have no ACEs, a child with five or more is seven to ten times more likely to develop drug addiction and turn to injection-drug use.[5] The study found definitively that the more trauma a child experiences, the more likely that child will abuse alcohol and other drugs.

So those in recovery who have experienced trauma, or think they have, are in good company.

Recovery can heal addiction, but the underlying wounds from child-hood remain, so healing childhood abuse and sexual trauma often re-quires professional care. Meanwhile, we can begin to look at some basic ways trauma colors so many people's early experiences with sex and drugs. For many people, entering recovery is the first time we speak about these childhood experiences—perhaps the first time we even remember them. Breaking silence and adopting recovery's practice of looking at the truth and speaking it out loud to at least one other person is a first step toward healing.

Once Upon a Time There Was a Little Girl . . .

One of the most common stories I've heard goes like this. A girl was mo-lested by an older man—her uncle, grandfather, stepfather, or her moth-er's boyfriend. Sometimes it was a boy molested by an older boy or a neighbor. The assaults began at age four or five or six and lasted until she was eleven or twelve or thirteen—from the times of earliest memory until she hit puberty and her body began to look like a woman's. The man either told her to do things to his body, or he did things to hers, or both. The girl then moves through adolescence and into adulthood only partly remembering—or allowing herself to remember—the things he did, but usually she remembers certain details of the scene extremely well: the pattern of his shirt; the smell of his tobacco or aftershave or sweat; or as Amy said earlier, "the exact way the room looked when he took me in there with him."

The girl tries her best to control her mind—to make the memories go away, or at the very least to ease their pain. In this way begins the habit of "dissociation," the psychological term for the separation of mind and body. We move out of the house because it's too painful to live there.

Then as she goes into puberty, other things happen. She may be allowed to see or hear something sexual with one or both of her parents, or out in the world. Diana, sixty-two, told me she'd been molested by her uncle from age six to eleven, and then at twelve years old she was walking to school when a guy pulled up in his car to ask for directions. "The entire time we were talking, he was masturbating," she said. "And I remember standing there giving him directions and thinking to myself, 'Wow—that guy has *a really big thumb!* And oh my god, *that thumb is getting even bigger!* And then it hit me: 'Oh—so *that's* what it looks like.' Because I had never seen one before." (Her uncle had done things to her body, so she hadn't seen his penis.)

"And the good news is," she said, "the guy didn't throw me into his car. He drove off, thank god. But then right after that, guess what—I got into big trouble at school and at home for drawing pictures of men with penises." She wasn't supposed to talk about any of this, because, by and large, we don't talk honestly and openly about sexuality with children, either at home or in our society—another reason she didn't know basic anatomy when the guy exposed himself. But how was this little girl supposed to live with the fact that her own body had been violated, and later that she'd seen a guy expose himself, without ever talking about any of it to anyone?

"So those were my first sexual experiences," she said simply. Before she ever had sex, as such, and before she ever drank or used any drug, her responses to sexuality were being distorted by the controlling, invasive sexual behaviors of adults around her.

Managing Post-Traumatic Stress with Lots of Sex and Drugs

The 2012 study of alcoholics also found that certain types of trauma result in higher rates of post-traumatic stress disorder (PTSD), especially in women, and that to survive this emotional stress, we look for solutions close at hand, including alcohol and other drugs. In a common variation of the story that I heard—not just in my work for this book but also in many, many meetings and talks with other women throughout nine years of working at recovery—this is what happens: girls start drinking, smoking weed, or using other drugs when they're fifteen, sixteen, seventeen—at about the time they start having sex. A lot of sex.

In the absence of opportunities to talk openly about it, girls control their feelings after trauma by having lots of sex, and by using alcohol and other drugs. Survivors of sexual abuse sometimes find themselves locked in a pattern of compulsive sex, according to sex educator Emily Nagoski. It's like biting on a cold sore or picking at a scab: you know the wound would heal faster if you'd stop fiddling with it, but picking at it—trying to manage it—becomes an irresistible urge, Nagoski writes.[6] "The result is that the survivor has multiple partners, often following a habitual pattern, without feeling perfectly in control of the decision to have those partners." But trying to control our feelings about sex by having a lot of it doesn't work. Just as trying to control our feelings by drinking and using doesn't work. Ah, Step One.

The ACE Study shows that adolescents do have compulsive sexual encounters to deal with how difficult—almost impossible, really—it is to try to cobble together a mature, "well-adjusted" sexuality out of the raw materials of early-childhood molestation and later exposure to inappropriate advances. And society compounds the problem by almost completely depriving children and adults alike of the language or opportunity for talking about our hurtful sexual experiences—to say nothing of language for our natural desires for sexual pleasure. We are obviously failing to protect many of our children from sexual abuse and then expecting them—we are expected, *we expect ourselves*—to live with the consequences without talking about it.

This is an absurd, destructive reality of our culture, and the stories in this book begin to change that.

Substitute Addictions: Sex Addiction and Food

What happens when survivors of early trauma detox and make it into recovery? The mind clears and the memories come back. And we no longer have substances to numb the memories' pain. So we sometimes substitute other addictive behaviors. Like compulsively having lots of sex.

Or compulsively not having sex at all, which is a hidden coping mechanism for controlling feelings called "sexual anorexia." In a culture that doesn't value talking honestly about sexuality—but which also commercializes sex to the point where you can buy images of it on any grocery store newsstand and order pornographic videos delivered to your phone—it's very hard to admit that you deal with your feelings by having *no sex at all*. But as Patrick Carnes, PhD, explains in his book *Sexual Anorexia*, having compulsive sex and engaging in sexual anorexia are two sides of the same coin.[7]

A more common substitute addictive behavior has to do with our relationship with food.

I was making tea and toast this morning at five-thirty, and as I was spreading honey and almond butter on my toast—with bread and toppings, a total of probably two hundred calories—I was thinking about how I'd made myself one piece of toast this morning instead of my usual two, because I'd recently gained three or four pounds. *Four pounds—* that's not even one hundred ounces. But my jeans are a little tighter than usual, and I've been watching how much I eat because I can feel the little belly I've put on. And I don't even have an eating disorder. I'm just an ordinary American woman, overly sensitive to any chub hanging on her bones.

I can't count the number of women in recovery who've told me that even before they began drinking, they started overeating, cutting back on food, or throwing up in order to control their feelings about early sexual trauma. But like having lots of sex, controlling our feelings by controlling how much we eat never works, partly because we can never entirely control our bodies.

Amy's story is a case in point. Her uncle began molesting her when she was four, and she started throwing up when she was about twelve or thirteen—at the beginning of puberty, shortly before the time she had her first drink. She was bulimic for five or six years, until she moved to college. When she moved from the suburbs to college in the city, her mode of transportation was walking. Which is a paleo thing—our bodies are evolved to walk long distances every day. Walking is a natural way to exercise for any member of *Homo sapiens*, even for a fit eighteen-year-old who was on her high school volleyball team.

She might have kept her body relatively fit, but she never really lived inside it. When she got to college, she started drinking in a more dedicated way, and then she started using other drugs, mainly benzos and heroin. At that point, she said, she found she no longer "needed" to throw up because she could numb out with drugs instead.

"Drugs were my cure for my eating disorder," she said. "They were the cure for the shame I carried from being molested."

When Amy chose recovery, she immediately started throwing up and starving herself again, and this triggered her obsession with alcohol and other drugs. "There were times in early sobriety when I was engaging in my eating disorder that I'd ask myself, 'I wonder what people who don't binge and purge do during early sobriety to not feel,'" she told me. "When I quit drinking and using, I simply could not operate in the world. I wanted to get out of my body, all the time." So she ate and threw up to distract herself from this intolerable state. And there was no way she could have a real sexual relationship in this internal conflict. She tried, but it was impossible to connect with the other person, just as it was impossible for her to truly connect with another person while she was drinking and using: she was too obsessed, too self-involved, too fearful.

"Now that I've dealt with my eating disorder in sobriety," she said, "I don't know how people maintain and sustain sexual relationships during an eating disorder. Because it's all-consuming. What was scary about my eating disorder, besides the fact that it was deadly, is that it made me feel so horrible about myself that I wanted to use drugs again."

I have spoken to women who have been sober and sexually abstinent for four, five, six, or even more than ten years who are survivors of trauma, who want to try having a relationship, but the trauma makes them afraid to let anyone touch them. One woman told me she'd been in recovery for drugs and alcohol for three years, and her last relationship was five years ago. During her recovery, she's had occasional flareups of the anorexia that had begun at sixteen but quieted during the years she drank and used. She feels quite comfortable being sexual on her own, but she sometimes worries she gets more pleasure from using her vibrators than she ever would with a person. "As much as I want a relationship, I do everything I can not to have one," she said.

She doesn't just need dating tips or advice about how to use Tinder. Her fear runs much deeper than that. "The thought of somebody touching my body, or seeing the inside of my home—there's all kinds of things that I don't want anyone to see. I'm totally self-sufficient. So part of me says, *If I don't find anyone, at least I'll still have good orgasms.* But that doesn't always cut it. I feel the loss."

Anorexia and bulimia are much more common in girls than in boys, but that doesn't mean men never use food to control their feelings. "Inside my addiction, I viewed myself as hideous," Tom told me. He had been molested by his mother and the guy who lived next door. "I made two decisions at a very young age," he said. "One, that I would not love or trust my mother; and two, that there was no god that could save me. The only thing I know to do—which is something I've seen my father and grandfather do—is eat through despair. So I get heavy, and I make myself ugly. I build a wall of fat around me. A lot of people say that only women do these things, but that's absolutely not the case."

It's important to keep in mind that just as with trauma, many eating disorders can be life-threatening and must be addressed professionally in conjunction with your substance addiction recovery program.

Allowing Ourselves To Be Vulnerable

It is said that the antidote to the shame of trauma—and shame in general—is vulnerability. As we grow in recovery, it's most often possible to experiment with vulnerability in the context of friendship.

One summer night last year I was invited to a party of women in recovery. I arrived to find about two dozen women, all in their early thirties or younger, gathered in the backyard around a bonfire. Small children were running around, and at fifty-one I felt like a grandma, watching out for the kids' bare feet near the bonfire and listening indulgently as the young women smoked and talked. For a while, I sat on the fringes of a small group who were discussing the nature of their orgasms. One young woman said (like so many other women I've talked with) that she was currently in the best relationship of her life and totally loved her partner, but was still not having orgasms during sex. Another young woman talked about how she'd had several spontaneous orgasms in a yoga class. All heads whipped around in her direction, including mine. "How many did you have? Who was the teacher? What position were you in? Was it *hot* yoga?" they asked.

"Being friends with women is the gift I've been given in sobriety," one of them told me. She had been raped during a blackout in college. "Having long-lasting deeper connections with other women is definitely a gift of recovery. It's so much easier to talk to other girls about what's going on in my life, including what's happening with my sexuality. We talk about sexuality all the time. We have to!—it's not like we're going to trust this stuff with just anybody. It's awesome that we can relate to each other, and maybe sometimes we can even give each other advice. But the best thing is that we can understand each other."

What Makes You Feel Good?

After publishing *Blackout,* Sarah Hepola researched and published a long feature story about the nature of sexual consent during alcohol blackouts.[8] It was a way to inquire into the feelings of confusion about whether she had consented to sex during her encounter as a thirteen-year-old girl with an eighteen-year-old man, and about all the blackout sex she'd had during her active addiction. Some people have urged her to label her first experience as rape, she said, and she seems less interested in categorizing that moment than in examining the twists and turns of people's experience, including her own.

"When I went back and listened to that tape of me at thirteen, I can go back and forth about whether it's rape, what his intent was," she said. "But to me the most jarring thing in the whole deal was that I had no sense of whether I liked this. Did I even want it? I carried that feeling with me through my thirties to the point where, when I got sober, I did not know what I liked in bed. I'd had lots of sex, and I made all the right sounds, but I did not know what I liked. The boyfriends I had would say things to me like, 'What do you want? What would make you feel good?' And I did not know.

"So I do think there's an opportunity to talk about what sexual trauma is. But I'm missing the question: What is sexual pleasure?"

We'll explore that in a later chapter.

. . .

Queries for Discussion

Trauma and Shame

☐ How did I learn about sex and sexuality? What words were used in my childhood for the body and its parts, for sensations, for feelings? How did these make me feel about my natural sexual inclinations?

☐ What words would I choose now for my own body and its parts, for my sensations and my feelings?

☐ How much do I allow media representations of male and female bodies to sway my feelings about my own body and about my sexual desire and response?

☐ Do I use my relationship with food for my enjoyment and health, or do I use food to manage unresolved feelings about past traumas?

☐ It's often said we're either moving toward or away from a drink or drug. How can I also understand myself moving either toward or away from shameful, judgmental attitudes about my sexuality?

☐ Do I allow myself to fantasize? If not, why not? How might I begin to experiment with fantasies that let me recover senses of sexual wholeness, excitement, adventure, peace?

THERÈSE

Choosing Pleasure Over God

Thirty-eight / Two years in recovery

I *really* don't want to give up having sex with Tony. But sometimes I feel like I have to. Because I feel like I've chosen Tony over God.

Tony and I have been dating for eighteen months. We met in recovery. At the meeting where we first saw each other, he asked whether he could hug me, and I was just really cold and bitchy and sort of rigid. I said, "I don't hug." I've been in recovery for ten years, and I'm working on three years of continuous time now. And whenever I've been sober, I've never been a hugger.

Sober, I'm very rigid. When I'm actually naked in bed with someone, I feel more free. And to get naked, I used to have to get drunk.

I knew how to behave when I was naked. I knew what to do in the bedroom. But I didn't know how to do the rest of the relationship. I didn't know how to be a girlfriend. I could do the bedroom thing, for my own pleasure. . . Well, to tell you the truth, not even for my pleasure. It was for their pleasure.

My pleasure was not the sex—it was just to be naked with somebody. Really what I wanted was just to be touched, to be held. So I would get drunk and get naked and do what I thought they wanted just so that I could be held. I was pretty, and at a party or in a room, I could find a guy that I wanted to be with, and he would be my prey—my challenge for the evening. To get him.

And then I'd get him. Get naked with him, in some form, somewhere.

That was the only way I knew how to get what I wanted. Which was just to be touched.

I was the last of eight children. My mother was a single mom. She had six children with one guy, and he left her for one of his employees. Then right away she went out and got pregnant by another guy who never stuck around. And then she got pregnant with me. She kicked my dad out when I was two because he had a drinking problem.

She was a super-devout saintly Catholic mom who went to church and was president of the Ladies of Charity, and yet the paradox was, she was a single mother. To me, at least, it seemed like a paradox. The Bible tells us that if we're going to be sexual and have kids and be able to maintain connection with God, we need to be married.

My mother basically gave up on men and put all her sexual energy into a garden. And it was a humongous garden, let me tell you.

After I had my third child eight years ago and kicked out Hugh—that's their father—I did the same thing. I made a huge "garden" out of pursuing school, work, and dreams. And I didn't have sex. For seven years before I met Tony, except for a couple of random times that weren't relationships, I wasn't sexual at all.

For one thing, I was terrified of getting pregnant. I mean, Catholics aren't supposed to use birth control, and this time with Tony is the first time in my life that I've actually used contraception. But even more than being afraid of pregnancy, I felt like I had to give up sex so I could be close to God. It was just a message I always got—that if I were having sex without being married, God would turn his face away from me.

Each time I got pregnant, I was trying to make my relationship with Hugh work. The last two times I got pregnant, I was sober. When we had sex, it was like we were playing Russian roulette: we didn't use contraception, and if we got pregnant, we thought it was "meant to be." I wanted to have children and a family with him. I wanted him to love me and take care of me, and I thought that was the way to get what I wanted.

I was fourteen when I lost my virginity. I was the last of all my friends. They'd all been doing it since they were twelve or thirteen.

And I started drinking when I was fourteen too.

I met my first love when I was eighteen. That's the first time I ever *made love*—where it felt loving and safe and all those wonderful things they say sex is supposed to be. But I didn't understand the dynamics of the relationship outside of the bedroom. So I dumped that guy because I felt like I didn't know how I was supposed to behave. It's not unusual, I think, to act that way at eighteen, but it really hurt him. He wouldn't forgive me. Sitting down and talking with him about how I treated him was a major amend I made in recovery.

After I dumped that guy, I saw dating and sex as a means to get what I wanted, which was to be touched and taken care of—whether it was financially, emotionally, socially, or physically. I had long-term lovers and they would provide for me, but I never loved them. I never let them touch my heart and spirit in the way my first love had. I would not allow it. I didn't want to hurt someone or be hurt by someone in that way again. My relationship served a purpose, but that purpose was never love.

The only time people would get remotely close to my heart was when I'd get drunk and take my clothes off with them. If I was naked in the room with somebody, the odds are I was drunk, and that was the only time I could open up.

Then I met Hugh.

I liked Hugh because he was strong. He was very physically powerful. He was a big, intimidating guy, and I was in awe of him. I loved to just watch him walk across a room. He sort of mesmerized me.

I was twenty-five, and I got pregnant right away. Even though he was pretty crazy, we moved in together, and everything got worse and worse. He controlled my movements, and he didn't allow me to see my friends. I stuck with it because I thought that was a part of my religious faith. In order to be a good person, I needed to stay with the father of my baby. But he was so mean, and he drank, and I drank too.

All my friends assumed I would have an abortion. That would be the automatic next step: I'm with this guy, and he treats me poorly, so obviously I'd do that. But all my life I've been taught that abortion is morally wrong. This was the first time I ran smack up against my upbringing—questioning my faith in God, questioning myself: *Do I believe in abortion? Is it possible for me to have one?*

I decided to have the baby, and it separated me from all my friends. I went from being a party girl to trying to be a mom.

I didn't quit drinking right away when I was pregnant. I'd just have like one drink. I once drank a beer in front of my friends, and they were horrified and judgmental. I was smoking, too, to be honest. I was more worried about the smoking. I just could not quit, and I felt a ton of shame about it.

The first time I left Hugh, I was *never* gonna go back!—right? I was that stupid once, and I was never gonna be that stupid again. Famous last words.

I would leave Hugh and then go back to him. Off, then on again. I was working at Safeway the whole time. I hated it. My nerves were shot. Hugh and I would fight, and at work when a customer yelled at me, I'd either want to kill them, or I'd stand there and cry. I went to work less and less, until I was working just one day a week.

Our sex life was never very good. Like, he didn't even kiss me while we were having sex. He loved me for the first two or three months of our relationship, and then he completely shut me out. I guess I stayed because I believed I deserved that treatment.

At one point in the middle of all this mess, I started going to a women's journaling group. I started writing in a journal every morning. And writing in that way unlocked my feelings. I'd wind up in a fetal position, crying over whatever I was writing that day. That's when I started doing the kind of internal work that needs to be done to recover from addiction. In writing whatever came to mind every day, I started to take an honest look at myself for the first time. That brought about my first spiritual experience. I quit drinking and tried to get honest with all the people around me.

But part of that spiritual awakening was also a belief in Jesus to a degree that was not healthy. I told myself, "Okay, the Bible is my guidebook, and I am totally willing to do whatever the Bible says to do."

I was convinced that meant I had to be with the father of my child. When you get right down to it, maybe the Bible doesn't really say that, but that was the message I always got when I was growing up. That was the paradox of my life: I was raised in this Catholic way but by a single mother. And I didn't want to be a single mother. But I was one.

After I had this spiritual experience, I decided I had to try to make Hugh want me by being what I thought he wanted me to be.

And meanwhile, on weekends, I was binge-drinking.

We had two more children. In the last couple years, there was no affection between us whatsoever. We were sleeping in separate bedrooms, and I got pregnant with my daughter when we had sex one night. Eventually I had to admit to myself it was an empty, ugly relationship. When my daughter was born eight years ago, I finally took the kids and moved out.

After I left Hugh, I decided I'd be sexually abstinent. For seven years I had only a couple of sexual slips. They weren't really *sex*—it was just, you know, oral sex. Which isn't really sex, right?

Being sexually abstinent all that time and at the same time trying to get sober taught me a lot of things. First of all, it taught me that I could get a lot of shit done if I didn't distract myself with men.

But even in terms of recovery, I learned so much by abstaining. You don't actually recover from drug addiction until you stop using, and in the same way, I think there was value for me in stopping having sex. For me it was about building a relationship with God.

I learned I have a very strong sexuality, and I feel protective of it, because now I see it as something valuable.

Toward the end of those seven years I started to feel like I wanted to try to be in a relationship with a man. So one weekend there was this big party, and beforehand I prayed to God and said, "If you think I'm ready for a relationship, please bring one into my life."

And at that party, Tony noticed me and pursued me all night. But I didn't go after him like prey, the way I used to do with men while I was drinking.

He has many of the qualities I want. He has a son, but his son isn't with him, and I wanted someone who understood parenthood but wasn't consumed by it. He was excited by the fact that I have kids, but he didn't want to have more. He wanted to be part of a family. And he's kind to me.

The only thing is, he was raised Catholic too, but he doesn't believe in Jesus the way I do. And I can't figure it out, but right now it just feels to me like I'm picking Tony over Jesus. I don't feel as close to Jesus because I'm in a sexual relationship outside marriage, which goes against what Jesus would like.

Maybe I would feel better if Tony and I got married.

We have really wonderful sex. It feels dreamy. He puts a lot of effort into learning how to please me—he actually researches things. He's really into it! Not in a goal-oriented way, but in a loving way. He's very loving, but at the same time it's very sexy. I mean, he kisses me all the time.

I could kiss all day.

He's loving outside the bedroom too. He came over last night and helped me move my furniture around my new apartment. He says "I love you," and I say "I love you," and we mean it.

So here I am, in the healthiest, most loving sexual relationship I've ever had, and I *still* don't feel pure or good enough! That sounds really screwed up, doesn't it? But I feel like I'm in sin. Part of me feels that we should get married because we love each other. And because I don't feel close to Jesus. When I was sexually abstinent, I felt very connected to God, all the time, every day.

I prayed to God to send me someone like Tony. So shouldn't that mean God must think it's okay that we're together?

At some point soon I feel like I'm going to have to choose either God or Tony. For me to be with Tony, I have to be sexual, because when we're near each other and we try not to be sexual, we can never manage it. We can't be alone together because we might have sex, you know? But if I'm sexual with Tony, then I'm choosing to cut myself off from God.

And the really crazy thing is, all this conflict I have in my mind goes away when we're actually having sex. When we're in bed, naked together, making love with each other, I never think I'm making any kind of sinful choice.

Except I can't have an orgasm. I've never had an orgasm with Tony.

In fact, the last orgasm I had with another person was probably at least twenty years ago. I'd still like to be strong enough to be abstinent from sex in my relationship with Tony. I may still try to go back to that. I miss feeling so close to God when I was walking in His will. I'm going on a retreat next week to fast and pray about it.

Touch

. . . .

His fingertips wove through her hair. "That feels so nice," she said, her face pressed against the humid skin of his neck.

"There's a word for that," he told her. "*Cafuné.*"

She asked him to repeat it slowly. "Kah, foo, neh," he said.

As he continued gently to wind his fingertips in her hair, she said, she fell asleep.

After she told me this story, I looked up the word "cafuné." It's apparently famous for being one of the world's words for which there is no English equivalent. It's a Brazilian Portuguese word for the act of running one's fingers through someone's hair with love and tenderness.

Sweet. Search a bit further, however, and you'll find sources that claim the word possibly originated in a previous century to describe the practice of adults running their fingers through their children's hair—to pick nits. This can seem super disgusting until you consider the evolutionary importance for primates of the habit of grooming. Primates—for example, gorillas, chimpanzees, and *Homo sapiens*—clean each other's skin from top to toe. And through touch, the skin (an enormous organ, at 15 to 20 percent of body weight) gives our minds more sensory information than any other organ except the brain.

In all primates, grooming is a daily social activity that can be one-way or mutual. Aside from promoting actual hygiene, grooming helps resolve conflicts, and it reinforces and restores trust. And yeah, it can enable one primate to let another know it's time to get it on.

"Grooming is a part of normal human life, even if we don't label it as such. Casual observation of people at home or in relaxed social settings reveals that most of us 'groom' one another regularly through touches, caresses, and reassuring pats and rubs," writes Nina Jablonski, PhD, professor of anthropology at Penn State, in her fascinating study of the human hide, *Skin: A Natural History*.[9]

Jablonski also writes that primates—including humans—who frequently groom each other show less anxiety and depression than primates who don't. I asked Jablonski about those who live alone, who may go days and days (sometimes much longer) with no physical touch. Would it be helpful for people, especially if they're trying to recover from addiction, to look for some way of being "groomed"?

"Touch has to be part of the comprehensive treatment of addiction," she said immediately. "Because you can change neurochemicals by taking drugs, but you can also alter brain chemicals through affecting systems that in turn affect the brain. For example, exercise and caring touch both release endorphins and reduce cortisol. And you can boost oxytocin through caring touch."

Let's review Jablonski's neurotransmitter name-dropping: Endorphins are the body's natural morphine. Cortisol is an anti-inflammatory steroid the adrenal glands release under stress (and with chronic stress, the adrenal glands can become exhausted). Oxytocin is nicknamed the "bonding hormone" or "cuddle chemical" because it's released in greatest amounts during breastfeeding and orgasm—but it can also be released through hugging, kissing, stroking the skin, or, for example, giving or receiving *cafuné*. Anything that lowers cortisol and elevates oxytocin has a good chance of lowering addiction relapse rates.

"You can say it's all neurochemical," Jablonski continued, "but in the case of exercise and touch, it's not neurochemicals delivered from outside the body through a pill. It's stimulating the body to produce its own neurochemicals. Because our bodies are very good at producing molecules that have positive psychoactive effects."

Which is another way of saying that our bodies are very good at healing by themselves—if we do the right things.

Psychologists have determined that when we humans don't get enough touch, we suffer from "skin hunger"—we starve for someone else to touch our skin. It's like it's encoded in our cells to want to be touched.

Which researchers like Jablonski think it may be, because of our primate genetics. It's well known that babies who don't get enough touch suffer from failure to thrive syndrome; but certainly adult humans also suffer when social mores, circumstances, or our own reticence deprive us of touch. Our skin becomes famished. The only thing that satisfies is some kind of "grooming."

Jablonski's research shows that people from some other countries seem to find it easier to satisfy this hunger before their skin becomes starved. "You see this in European countries, Italy for instance, a lot more touching between same-sex individuals, between people when they see each other, or even if they don't know each other. Prolonged holding of hands, not just a sterile handshake," Jablonski said. "Our culture is an exception. Most Western cultures engage in far more touching than American, English, and Germanic cultures, which are remarkably touch-averse. We are suffocating from American media. Whether you're looking at American movies or TV or news, you're basically looking at American habits of physical spacing and lack of contact. Those are widely disseminated throughout our own country and elsewhere."

"In a country like Brazil"—where *cafuné* is a thing—"you're just going to have a different pattern of socialization, and it's very, very healthy and much more representative of our species."

"The problem is," Jablonski mused, "how do you allow caring touch to be more of an accepted part of addiction treatment when it is seen as a potentially risky behavior that leaves people open to physical, sexual, or psychological abuse? This is an area where nothing has been worked out. Institutions are so risk-averse. They say, 'In theory this may be a good idea, but we can't figure out an implementation, so we have to withhold on this.'"

Psychologist Tiffany Field, PhD, who directs the Touch Research Institute at the University of Miami School of Medicine, has been trying to study the effects of massage on heroin users, given heroin's resurgence in south Florida, but she cannot get funding even from the National Institute on Drug Abuse. It seems that funders (many of which are tied into the big pharmaceutical companies) would rather study what you can put inside your body to change your neurochemicals, rather than what happens when you support the body's own healing processes. Field, who is recognized by Jablonski and others as the nation's foremost expert on human touch, said that despite the formidable healing capacities of touch, nobody can get funding to study its effects in addiction treatment.

Is there any medication you can take, I asked Field, that simulates the benefits you get from caring touch? "I don't know of any medication," she said. "I don't really know what would substitute for touch."

I don't know the answers to the question about incorporating touch into addiction treatment. Some treatment centers have begun offering massage, acupuncture, and other neuro-somatic modalities as part of their programs. And that proves Jablonki's point, the fact that these treatments are called something other than just plain "human touch."

Or *cafuné*. If I had to pick a treatment center, I would pick the one that offered daily *cafuné*.

The Kiss

Can there be a more intimate and caring form of touch than a kiss?

Nobody knows for sure how kissing evolved. It's not necessary for procreation, so why do we do it? Some hypothesize it came from an ancient practice of chewing food for our babies, then transferring it to their mouths directly from our own. Some think it might have been a natural extension of our primate ancestors' practice of sniffing each other's skin, either to determine the genetic makeup of a potential partner, or just to check that we've come back to the right partner. (Or, in my amateur opinion, just to enjoy the pleasure of your partner's scent, the way you might sniff your baby's head by rubbing your lips against his scalp.)

A kiss is a way of exploring inside someone else's body. Our lips touch each other's. Our tongues venture inside each other's mouths. Mucous membranes exchange cells. Taste buds and teeth create friction; saliva makes the whole thing slip and slide.

Kissing is not just about touching the other person. We smell their skin, we hear their breath, we taste, we feel their responses. Tongue and lips are built dense with nerve cells. So are the ears; so is the nose. Cells ignite; synapses flash with the same electricity that enlightens the world during a thunderstorm.

All that energy—in lightning, in bodies—comes from the sun. In eating food, we eat our star; in kissing each other, the body sparkles inside.

We feel excitement, enjoyment, hope, affection.

Where do feelings reside? In the carbon and oxygen of our flesh, and in other places besides. Feelings are not just contained in the brain. The body has more than one brain, anyway.[10]

Kissing awakens feelings and makes them move. Thus the word "emotion."

A kiss is more than strictly a physical or material action. It's not just smashing one's lips against the lips of another person (although sometimes it can be that). We breathe with and against and into each other. The other person's exhalation becomes our inspiration.

Sex is fluid. Its range is much wider and deeper than just the acts of taking off clothes, touching each other between the legs ("foreplay"—such an inadequate word), inserting tabs into slots, coming to climax.

Sex's territory, thanks to evolution—or to J.C., Allah, Yahweh, or the Wiccan mother-goddess[11]—encompasses the vast, varied, and enchanted land of kissing.

*   *   *

Queries for Discussion

Touch

☐ How long has it been since someone else last touched my skin?
How long has it been since I gave someone else a loving touch?

☐ What are the differences between the way touch felt to me when
I was using alcohol or other drugs and the way it feels now that
I'm in recovery? Did drugs in some ways make touch feel safer?
Does it now feel more intense, and if so, how do I feel about that
intensity?

☐ How much and what kinds of physical touch do I need, want,
and like? Give specific examples (such as "I need someone to
hold my hand," or "I like it when someone holds the back of my
neck while hugging me").

☐ How can I bring more touch into my life and into others' lives?
What are some ways I can get the kinds of touch I need? Which
people in my life do I trust enough to ask them to exchange these
kinds of touch with me?

☐ What feelings or events in my history might hold me back from
receiving or giving touch?

LINDA

Reaching Out with No Expectations

Sixty-six / Twenty-two years in recovery

My thirty-two-year-old daughter is dating this guy, and she said to me, "I don't understand why it's not working out. We both want the same things." I said, "Look, just because you want the same things doesn't mean he's the right guy. Do you like him as a person? Does he challenge you? Or does he second-guess everything you say? You can speak up and say what you want in the relationship."

I can give her this advice now because I'm clean and sober. She was ten when I came into recovery. I'd kept my mouth shut with men for so many years. I was the best orgasm faker on the planet. And orgasm wasn't the only thing I faked. I picked my second husband because, on paper, we looked like the perfect couple. We had limos taking us to dinner. We had a tri-level house in Beverly Hills and we looked like Barbie and Ken. On paper it looked sweet, but in real life he made me so miserable. He was controlling and made me cry every time we sat across from each other in a restaurant. But I put up with it because I'd learned I had to be grateful that once again a man had rescued me.

I put up with it because what it looked like on paper was more real to me then than what it felt like inside me.

Back in the day, when I was a hippie chick, I'd take my clothes off at the drop of a hat. I guess you would have called me a free spirit. I just didn't give it that much thought. Of course, all that tequila lowered my inhibitions considerably.

I was forty-four and single when I got sober, and I was so self-conscious about my body. Let's just say, I've never had tiny ballerina boobs. I was middle-aged and not drinking and I couldn't *imagine* taking my clothes off with somebody without a having drink or a line. My husband, Jimmy, he's known me for almost thirty years, and not even *he* has ever seen all of me naked—he just thinks he has. I'm telling you, *nobody's* seen my butt in forty years because I've learned how to walk out of the room backwards! Jimmy sleeps naked, and I still sleep in pajama pants and a tank top.

I think I've started to turn this perfectionistic attitude around by raising my daughter in sobriety. She has big, bright stretch marks. She just doesn't give a shit. She accepts herself. She's like, "If somebody doesn't like me because of my stretch marks, that's not somebody I want to be with."

I was the screwup in the family because I got pregnant right out of high school, which shouldn't have happened, because we were the first generation who had birth control. I grew up in a big family in a small Southern town in the fifties, and when your parents gave the clear impression that you're the family screwup, well, hell!—that's almost like a lethal blow: everyone in town was talking about me.

My son, Trey, was born in 1967 right here in Austin, and I gave him up for adoption. Before I got sober, every year on his birthday I'd just get loaded. It would be my sole goal.

I was in the rooms for a couple years before I started telling the truth about the fact that I wanted to find him. At a meeting a woman told me about searchers who find adopted kids. I sent this agency three hundred dollars, and within two hours they had my son's name and address. Turned out he was still living in Austin. They contacted him and told him who I was. He was twenty-seven, and he didn't want to know anything about me. He had a good life, so I felt I had to leave him alone and accept the truth: he didn't want to know who I was.

Before, when I was drinking and using, I'd have pulled the drunk-dialing act or shown up on his doorstep.

Instead, I talked about it in meetings. And it continued to remain on my mind—I finally knew where my son was, and he and I were both in Austin, but I couldn't see him or talk to him. And it was like I had to give him up all over again. The grief washed over me: I had to let him go. I had to surrender. I had to accept that I couldn't control the situation. But this time, I had people who cared about me to support me.

A friend of mine knew the high school where he'd gone. She tracked down one of their yearbooks and ripped out the page with his picture so I could know what he looked like. I pored over that photo. I wanted to call him, I wanted to camp out on his doorstep, and if I'd been using, I would have. It was hard, but I left him alone. I prayed to be given the strength to do that.

And then one day I was at the gym sweating my butt off on an elliptical and this guy ran by me on the track, and I said to myself, *That's my son.*

I told myself, *Be careful. Don't be crazy. Maybe your imagination's carrying you away.* And then he got on a bike across from me so I could see his face, and his eyes were exactly like mine. I mean, it was *him.* My son. I hadn't laid eyes on him in nearly thirty years, since I gave him up when he was three days old.

So I went to the receptionist, who was a friend of mine, and I told her what I'd just seen. I was shaking like hell. She said, "We're going to do this right now. We're going to introduce you to your son."

And she walked me over and introduced the two of us. We talked to each other for a little while. He was smiling at me. We talked for a few minutes, and eventually we said goodbye.

And then nothing. For *years.* Several years went by and I heard nothing from him. Every year I'd send him a birthday card. My friends in recovery told me to be patient—that it was all working out the way it needed to. The people at the search agency told me to just keep reaching out from time to time without any expectations.

They told me to send him a letter telling him where I was when I lost him.

Well, I couldn't do that, could I? I couldn't tell him how he was conceived and why I had to give him up.

I'd been sending Trey invitations to family gatherings, but he never acknowledged them. One year my husband Jimmy and I were just arriving at a big family reunion when my phone rang and this voice said, "Linda, it's Trey."

So he showed up that day at the reunion and spent the whole afternoon. I had sent him a DVD with photos of our family, and he called me that night and we talked on the phone while he looked through all the pictures.

And then as I continued to let it be and accept that I could not control the situation, slowly he started getting in touch with me online.

You know how, when you get clean, they give you that stupid direction to make a list of what you want and not shortchange yourself? And you're like, "Get lost—I'm just happy with what little I have." Having a relationship with my son was on that list, but I couldn't really let myself have that desire. I was like, "Get lost—I'm not gonna put it on this list, because I just cannot get hurt again." I had no idea that this desire could be fulfilled.

But today, it is. My son and I talk once or twice a week. And he tells me he loves me, and I get to tell him I love him. I got to meet his parents, and they hugged me and *thanked* me.

I'm really not a religious person, and I hardly ever say stuff like this, but you know what—it's a miracle.

Once when Trey came to see me, Glenn—my old high-school boyfriend, the boy I believe to be Trey's father—showed up with one of his sons. Trey didn't like Glenn at all. He was so angry his father had abandoned me. Anybody who banishes their parents—it's their choice to let you go, but when you hear your flesh and blood say, "I don't want to know you, because you did such-and-such"—it's just going to affect you.

I told Glenn, "You just have to accept him for where he's at."

That's a principle I learned to live by in recovery: acceptance. That's the kind of thing your parents should teach you, but most parents don't even know it themselves. When we make it into recovery, we get to pass that on.

I've forgiven Glenn. He has said to me, "I wasn't there for you," and the only way I could forgive him was to accept the fact that he just wasn't capable of making a commitment. And in that acceptance, I became a little bit more free.

Trey was told I dumped him in the hospital when I was eighteen and that I danced down the corridor as I left the building.

I've told him I wanted to keep him. I've told him I'd wanted to marry his father and that his father left me. But I haven't told him why Glenn left—why I had to give him up. I just can't do that. I pray about it, but I don't know whether I'll ever have the strength to do that.

When I gave birth to Trey, the hospital staff gave me the option to let him go without holding him, but I stayed with him in the hospital for three days. And then I let him go. It was right after the tornadoes of Hurricane Beulah annihilated my hometown. Until I got sober and started therapy, I didn't realize how much traumatic stress I'd endured that year.

I was fortunate that I was sober and in therapy when I remembered the rapes. A lawyer had asked me out—he was a rising star in LA, where I was living then, and I said I'd go out with him. And that night he raped me. I had bruises on my neck and arms.

The next day he actually called and asked me out again. He said, "I really had fun."

I tried to wash off what he'd done to my body. I took a bath with my favorite bath oil, which I'd used ever since I was a teenager. When I poured it into the tub, I started to remember the rapes when I was seventeen—I'd bathed in it one night before I went drinking with a bunch of Glenn's friends, some of them older. We'd all gotten wasted, and they forced themselves on me.

When those memories came back, I called Glenn and asked him about that night. He said, "I thought you knew that's why I didn't marry you."

This was the mid-sixties, and those good ol' boys were people he admired. One was like a father figure to him. Glenn told me they'd bragged to him, "We got Linda last night!" He didn't have the guts back then to talk with me about it. He was ashamed that all his friends had screwed me all at once, and he pulled away from me.

But there we were, both in our forties and talking about it. It was pretty powerful.

I had found my son in the mid-nineties, and he didn't show up to that family reunion till 2005. For *ten years* I'd been practicing letting it go, taking it back, letting it go again. And I talked about it so much with my home group. Jimmy also helped me. After I got sober, I couldn't drink my way through Trey's birthday anymore. One year, I was at Jimmy's house, and he said, "Why don't we try to *celebrate* his birthday this year? Let's have some people over for dinner. We won't tell them what it's for, but we'll have a cake and everything." Jimmy's love helped me accept my feelings. He helped me accept that I wanted to find my son and have a real relationship.

I couldn't have lived through that time of finding my son if I hadn't had all these people who love me. I couldn't have practiced acceptance like that. My goal is that in this family someday we will all know the whole truth, and we will accept it, and we'll all move forward. I feel confident in my relationship with my son. Now we know each other, we're not just two strangers, and he appreciates me. He tells me he loves me. He loves my daughter. He's an amazing person.

But I think if he found out the truth about how I had to give him up . . . I'm not comfortable enough yet to risk telling him. I don't have *that* much acceptance. Yet.

I've had boyfriends in sobriety. I've even had nice boyfriends. But they were always "program boyfriends." I'd never dated anybody who wasn't in recovery. It was actually easier for me to date inside the program, because I was going to a lot of meetings. I didn't meet a lot of men who weren't in recovery. And

I mean, the reality is, down here in Texas, if you dip your toe across the county line, you come across guys with Confederate flags and guns in their trucks.

Jimmy's "normal." Meaning he drinks around me, a beer here and a beer there, and he's exactly how he was when I was dating him years ago. Jimmy knew me at my messy, drunken worst and he still loves me and he accepts me for who I am.

We started dating in 1988. I was living in New York and still drinking and using and coming down here to visit him. He'd never been married before, he was coming out of a long relationship, and we had sort of an open arrangement. We broke up and stayed friends, and then I got sober and moved back here. When I had five years, and we were still good friends, we were talking on the phone one day and I told him I felt like I hadn't had sex since Eisenhower was president, and he said, "Same here."

So we said, "We trust each other. Why not?" And we got together.

We'd been best friends for years. For the first time in my life, I wasn't identifying myself as being in a relationship. Being sober, I said to him after a while, "Look, if you want a monogamous relationship, that's what I want."

I'd never done that before—just *said* what I wanted.

Four years ago we got married. This is my third marriage and his first. He's sixty-eight. We have a duplex, which I'd just bought when we started seeing each other again. We sleep on his side and we eat on my side.

I'm lucky in that Jimmy's sexual capacity matches mine really well. When we got back together, we were having sex three or four times a week. Now we go through periods of time when we don't have sex at all. At the longest, it's maybe a month. He's probably more interested than I am. If we haven't had sex in a while, he'll mention it to me, and I'll realize, "Oh my god, you're right!"

I guess our ideas of what's pleasurable kind of match. We've been married for only four years, but we've known each other for more than three decades. We're just comfortable with each other.

Pleasure

. . . .

When I was on a ton of painkillers, it was hard for me to feel sexual pleasure. I rarely wanted sex, and I had lots of trouble having orgasms. The fact that I couldn't come worried me, and I strategized to see if I could fix the problem. My approach was to do what Charlotte did in that *Sex and the City* episode where she holes up in her apartment one entire weekend with her vibrator.[12] Thinking (naturally) that all my solutions came from outside me, I told myself, *That's the answer—I need that vibrator.* Not just a vibrator, but *that one.* As if a sitcom could solve any problem for me, I ordered Charlotte's rabbit-vibrator toy.

What my little experiment taught me was that this battery-powered silicone miracle machine with rotating pearls and twitching ears could not give me pleasure, even when I cranked it onto the highest setting. My body was too numb. But I also discovered that if I were at any level of withdrawal from the painkillers, I could have multiple orgasms.

I'd never had multiple orgasms before. I basically thought they were an urban legend. (Some scientists also think they're an urban legend. See the chapter on Sexual Surrender for more about what a neuroscientist told me about multiple orgasms.) So I kind of didn't believe in them— that is, until I had my first bunch of three or four. Finding out I could have multiple orgasms became an incentive for me to quit drugs and get into recovery. But my Catholic upbringing got in the way: a big part of me still thought my strong sexual response made me dirty. My mother raised me to think of sex as sinful until somehow, with the flick of a holy switch somewhere, it became okay during marriage. To use the words of Joe and Charlie, the late leaders of renowned Big Book workshops, she'd taught me it was "a dirty filthy rotten thing . . . and you should save it for the one you love."[13] I empathize with Thérèse, who tells a story in this book about feeling she has to choose between Jesus and her boyfriend. People have names for sex outside marriage: "premarital sex" and "fornication," or "adultery"—terms I've never used with my own son, but I've inflicted them on myself. For many of us, from earliest memory, human sexual response has been tied up and weighed down with negative labels and judgments.

In the end, my sexual response shone a light to guide my way. The discovery that my body could experience much more pleasure than I'd imagined was life-altering. In my active addiction, with my suppressed sexuality, I'd begun to feel that maybe I was killing a part of myself that was normal, natural, and good, a part that had been given to me at my creation—a kind of life-force.

After I detoxed, post-acute withdrawal syndrome knocked me flat for a long time. Still, I could feel my sexual desire. And I didn't know how to handle that, partly because I had totally hidden my worry about my lack of response from my then husband. All of a sudden, for the first time in my adult life, I had lots of desire for sex. But like some of the women in this book, I wasn't used to having sex without manipulating my responses with drugs. Also, like many women in this society, I didn't think the purpose of sex was to please me. I thought my job in bed was to please my partner—another way of approaching sexuality that I'd learned growing up in my Catholic family. "I don't need to come," I'd say. I said it so much for so long that by the end of my addiction, I had convinced both of us.

Such intense pleasure, and the desire for pleasure, is a sign that our bodies are healing. It's the numbness that's part of the sickness. "When I was drunk, there was something so barreling about me. There's no nuance. So much of sex is about the softness, the light touch, the pleasure," Sarah Hepola, author of *Blackout*, told me. "But toward the end, I was having guys pull my hair. Part of that desire for roughness was a desire for sensation, because I had numbed myself out so much. When you were as drunk as I was, when you have sex, you've anesthetized yourself, even though these are the most sensitive parts of your body. I really felt like,

'Push me against the wall. Throw me over the bed. Pull my hair.' I liked people being rough with me."

When we drink and use, sometimes we numb ourselves for so long that we don't know what would really please us. When we get sober, we may have a lot to learn about what kinds of pleasure we like.

Numbing Pleasure and Other Feelings

People who don't understand addiction think we used drugs to feel pleasure. People who understand addiction know that we often used drugs to numb our feelings. But neither we nor the drugs are smart enough to choose which feelings to numb. Pain and pleasure are just two sides of one coin, so along with numbing the pain of feelings like fear and anger, we also numb feelings of pleasure.

What exactly is pleasure, anyway? Sex educator Emily Nagoski says, simply, "It's what feels good." Pleasure is not the same as sexual desire, which Nagoski says is often mistakenly used as a measure of sexual well-being. Desire is psychological, but pleasure is physical: our body's ability to feel and enjoy sensations. "Pleasure is the single best measure of sexual well-being we've got," Nagoski writes on her blog. "Pleasure is the measure. Focus on sensation, and do more of what feels good, less of what doesn't feel good."[14]

To be a bit more specific about what it means when we talk about what we "feel": there are sensations, as Nagoski notes, and then there are the stories we tell ourselves about those sensations. For example, if I were to stick my hand over a candle flame, I might do two things:

- I feel the burn. That's the *sensation.*

- I start almost immediately to tell myself the story of the burn. I label it: I say it hurts, I'm in pain, I'm suffering. Pain and suffering are feelings. But then I start building feeling on feeling, story on story: "This burning feeling might never end. I better never do this again." And worse: "What an *idiot!* I should be *ashamed* of myself. I *hate myself.*"

It might feel awesome to use a drug to numb the feelings that come from the story we tell ourselves about the sensation. But using a drug would also numb any sensation of pleasure we might feel.

To give an example in the sexual realm: I go on a date, we're attracted to each to each other, and we go back to my place and start making out. I might do two things:

- I might feel super turned on. My heart might be racing and my skin might be flushed. I'm *hot*. That's the sensation.

- Then I tell myself the story of the sensation. I label it: "I don't know this person well. This is a *hookup*. I feel *ashamed*." Shame is a feeling. But instead of inquiring into the shame and trying to let go of the judgment behind it, I allow it to control me by labeling myself: "*Good* people don't have one-night stands. I must be *bad*."

We sometimes hear people say, "I used drugs because they worked, until they didn't anymore." Drugs actually work. They numb feelings so we don't have to inquire into them. They distract and make us not care about the stories our minds write. They stop working when the pain of the damage they wreak outweighs their benefits. In active addiction, that damage shows up in distortion of the truth like the ones illustrated above, and in obsession about the drugs on which we've come to rely as our solution to the unexamined feelings. And the damage also includes all the harm the drugs do to the tissues of the body.

So it's important to learn how to inquire into our feelings rather than numbing them out. Shame and judgment are some of those "old ideas" that we have to let go of absolutely, or the result will be nil. It's better to look into the shame and talk with somebody about it, and Steps Four and Five can help us do that.

Practicing Sensitivity

We can train our minds to drop the shame and judgment about our feelings and instead to pay attention to the sensations and feelings themselves. When we practice this kind of mindfulness, we learn that the sensations and feelings change, and we prepare ourselves to make conscious decisions that are wiser and more in line with our values. But for people with addiction, meditation—which trains us to pay attention to sensation—is a freaky proposition. Our obsessive habits make us want to jump in and control it with this, that, or the other substance. Recovery asks us to practice accepting our feelings and allowing them to pass. We turn to Step Eleven. When we meditate, we practice watching our sensations change and our feelings come and go. When a feeling takes a long time to pass, we practice a version of Step Twelve: we help someone else by asking for their help. Sometimes the message I carry to another person with addiction is, "The monsters are out of the closet today—can you remind me that they're just the ghosts of my addict mind passing through?"

"I hope you can find a way to tolerate your life being up in the air, or even to enjoy it," a friend with thirty years wrote me the other day after I confessed to him some of my fears. "I find it can be quite enjoyable to be up in the air, as long as I don't worry too much about how I'm going to land."

If obsession and distortion of the truth are sentinel aspects of life in addiction, these practices lead to a sentinel aspect of life in recovery: the sense that no matter what the outcomes, no matter how we land, everything will be all right.

Learning to Stay Inside Feelings

Substance abuse keeps us from experiencing our sexual feelings in many ways. Some women I talked with mentioned having sex during blackouts and waking up either in the middle of the act or afterward in a strange person's bed. Then there were the men I talked with who told me about paying for sex, watching porn, and having sex with strings of partners during their addictions to prove they were super masculine. And there were heroin and painkiller users who talked about their total lack of interest in sex.

Some people also mentioned that they learned to shut off their feelings during sex—losing connection not just with their partners but also with themselves. As we learned in the chapter on trauma, this is called "dissociation," and it can occur among people with unhealed experiences of sexual abuse in their early histories. But it can also come from growing up in an alcoholic family, or just from growing up in a super addictive and disembodied culture. "People with addiction feel everything so strongly, and sex is one of the strongest things you can feel," said Rosalyn Dischiavo, a certified sex educator with thirty-three years in recovery from addiction. "If you grew up in an alcoholic family, you might have learned it was dangerous to have or express feelings."

The list of stuff we've *heard* about sex is endless: Guys want sex more than women do; men like casual sex better than committed sex and oral sex better than *any* other kind; sex with the same person is doomed to become boring; oral sex prevents STDs; big feet mean a large . . . From our earliest days, hearsay about sex shapes what we think and how our bodies and minds respond when other people touch us, and when we think about touching them. These shameful messages can make it even harder for us to stay inside our feelings of pleasure.

Because our society discourages honest discussion about sex and sexuality, we preternaturally pick up the ideas that sex is shameful and that we have to hide our sexual experimentation, especially if we identify as something other than hetero. Everyone I talked with who claimed any sexual fluidity at all said they felt they had to hide. And I'm not just talking about people of my generation who grew up in the 1970s; I'm talking about people who got sober as teenagers and now they're only twenty-four.

Hiding is painful in and of itself, and for those of us with addiction, hiding becomes a painful way of life. As a result, many of us women make it into our thirties, forties, or beyond without knowing, for example, where our own clitoris or "G-spot" is. If we do know where they are, we may not know how to stimulate them ourselves, much less how to educate our partners about what stimulation we like. The truth is, whether we're men or women, when we start to recover we might not even know what we ourselves like. Imagine waking up at, say, thirty-five, forty, or forty-five, sober, and not knowing what turns you on. Lots of folks start drinking and using in their teens at least in part because they have no clue how to negotiate sex and they're just plain nervous. But if you're forty and you wake up sober without the first clue what you like sexually, you might feel more than a little nervous.

Hell, you don't even have to be that old to feel super-nervous about having sober sex. A twenty-four-year-old woman told me she didn't start wanting sex until about six months into recovery, when she ran into a guy she'd known and thought was cute. "We went on a date and had sex," she said.

"What did you find out?" I asked.

"That I could do it," she said. "I really didn't even know if I could do it!"

Any kind of nervousness is often what makes teens drink or take drugs in the first place: to relax and fit in, or to hide.

"Feeling okay about how you feel—even when it's not what you expected—is the key to extraordinary sex," Emily Nagoski emphasizes. But so many of us don't feel okay about how we feel, during sex or at other times. What *other* reason was there to start drinking or using at age seventeen, thirteen, nine, or even younger?

No scientist has pinpointed whether or how sexual response is connected to the development of addiction, Nagoski told me. What we do know, she said, is that people with addiction have "sensation-seeking" temperaments. If you put headphones on a person without addiction and turn up the volume, the brain activity decreases. But in people with addiction, the opposite happens—the more stimulation, the more our brain activity increases.

We move *toward* the drama. And when our feelings tell us "Too much!" we don't know how to turn down our super-sensitive nervous systems—at least, not on our own.

Sex and Attachment

People with addiction frequently have had interrupted or otherwise insecure attachments to people who were supposed to make them feel safe, Nagoski said. This makes sense given the statistics about the prevalence of people in recovery who have experienced trauma. It's the feeling of safety and trust that turns down the noise and helps us be honest.

"Insecure attachment is really common among people with addiction history," Nagoski says. "Your body doesn't know for sure that if the object of your attachment goes away, they're going to come back. Your body copes with this situation by becoming anxious, and grabbing on really hard and never letting go, and you feel like you're going to die. Or else it becomes avoidant—you cope by never attaching to anyone very strongly." Which also eventually makes us feel like we're going to die. And which also means it's important for us in recovery to find a community of people who make us feel safe enough to learn how to trust each other and ourselves, who teach us to stay inside our feelings, and who help us learn to turn down the volume on the noise and drama.

Nagoski is one of the most compassionate and sensible people I've ever talked with about sex. Her attitude is entirely accepting of the gamut of human variation in desire, response, orientation. It's that kind of acceptance that I want to keep cultivating for myself. That acceptance is also called *love*, and if I can't give that to myself, then no amount of sex with any other human being is going to give it to me. That's one thing I learned when I made recovery my priority before everything, including my sexual relationships.

To love myself, I have to inquire deeply and honestly into my feelings. Which means I have to communicate with the same honesty—first with the various parts of myself that I buried with my addiction, and then with other people in my life. Getting honest is the topic for our next discussion.

· · ·

Queries for Discussion

Pleasure

☐ Am I familiar with my own anatomy? Do I understand the anatomy of my partners? How comfortable am I just using my own senses to explore my body for pleasurable zones and responses? How comfortable am I with asking a partner what's pleasurable and what's not?

☐ If I were to visit a sex educator or doctor to ask questions about sexual response, what questions would I ask?

☐ In what situations have I engaged in sex—in addiction and in recovery—as a way to escape other feelings? Have I used sex as a drug? Have I been honest with my support people and recovery community about my actions in these situations? Who do I trust enough to talk with about these experiences?

☐ What originally turned me on sexually before I began using and drinking?

☐ What do I want or like in sex that I don't ask for? What feelings or events in my history keep me from asking for this pleasure?

☐ Did I learn not to ask for what I want or like? In what ways might I be able to go about finding out?

☐ If I were to invest the time and money I spent on drugs and alcohol in exploring my own capacity for honest pleasure, how might I invest those resources?

☐ Have I attempted to manipulate others through sexual behavior? In what ways may I have tried to use sex to distance myself from emotional attachment?

DRÉ

What Is True Respect?

Thirty-four / Ten months in recovery

I was born into drug use. In my family it was cute to give alcohol to a baby. My grandmother used to say, when a baby is teething?–you take alcohol and rub it on his gums.

My mom raised me on her own. She the *queen.* I mean, that woman is a *trooper,* man, she been with me every step of the way. Now that my mind's clear I can understand and *see* the love of a mother toward her son. It's–it's *unwavering.*

But she worked, and she worked hard, so she had to leave me in the care of other folks. My father, he's still alive, but I don't know the man. And my mother had other kids after me. By my mother I have one younger brother–he's doing really well, driving eighteen-wheelers, just got his license. And I have a half-sister who's also doing well.

My drinking began when I was around eleven years old. I guess at eleven it was experimentation. When I was thirteen, it began to be continuous. Less experimentation and more a way to get through what each day brought.

I started being interested in girls around nine or ten. In puberty, things are going on in your body, hormones are raging, you're experimenting with yourself. My first sexual experience was at fourteen. I didn't have sex all the way till I was seventeen, so at fourteen it was just some fooling around, but still, I didn't do it for the girl or for me. I did it to earn the respect of the men in my family. Uncles, cousins–you know, it was the kind of household where it's one big house, and the family comes and goes. At that age, I sort of idolized those men, even though they'd done some things and were in and out of prison. To win their approval, I can remember coming home after that first experience—they slapped my hands and congratulated me.

I wanted to live up to what those men in my family expected, and I used that as an excuse to justify a lot of my behavior, but a person can't give what they don't have, right? They didn't have that so-called image of a strong man to give. Because doing what they done ain't really being a strong man, but I didn't know that then. Since I was just a kid, the only thing I knew to do was to try and be like them. So at thirteen or fourteen, for me to put my hand around a bottle of beer and drink it, and say that I can do it, and acting crazy, and the other guys saying, "Yeah! He a man now!"—that's what I thought growing up meant. I thought that was what earning respect meant. So I wanted to keep doing that.

Last night at a meeting we was talking about fear. And for me, being fearful was a way of life. I felt I was unacceptable to the men that raised me, you know? At the meeting I gave 'em an example, like—there was bullies, neighborhood bullies—this one guy especially who I was no match for—and I was scared to go to school and be around 'em. But instead of dealing with it myself, I let my uncles and cousins find out, and they went and dealt with the bullies. But then I caught shit at home for not being able to deal with them my own self. So I learned I'd rather deal with the bullies than deal with the guys back home. It made me feel like I wasn't strong enough to do it myself. Deep inside, I lost respect for myself, because I didn't want to be like the men in my family.

Come to find out, the guy I was no match for?—he didn't have no confidence neither.

So now I want to embody that *real* confidence. I always wanted that. Because believe it or not, in here? Deep inside? I'm just a softie. The kind of lifestyle I was living, in and out of prison, I can't go on like that.

And this I know—if I don't pick up a drink or a drug, I ain't going to jail.

First girl I ever met who I really liked, I was thirteen. She was ten.

It was puppy love. Love-at-first-sight type of thing. From the point when I met her, I knew I wanted to marry her. We thought the same way, you know what I'm saying?

We were friends. We never had sex. We never got that intimate. I would say that, throughout my life, the respect I was able to show in any other relationship, for any other woman, was due to her.

Through everything that happened later, I always figured in the back of my mind I'd make my way back to her. But the decisions I made pushed me further and further away from her. Breaking in cars, stealing, fighting—being in and out of jail, starting with juvenile jail. And then later, other stuff. I been in prison more times than I can count, usually for drug-related offenses.

In the lifestyle I used to live, I had a certain identity of myself and knew what I wanted. So I physicalized women: if she looks good enough to be with me, that's it, I'm gonna go for it. I didn't really look at her inner qualities. And as a single mother, my mom had tried to tell me about sex, but it was nothing like having a man around to really sit with me and tell me about it. The men in my family basically taught me to use as many women sexually as I could, so to speak. And that's how I identified as a man—how many women I used. So I was set out on the wrong course.

But I knew in my heart what real love was because of this girl I'd met when I was thirteen. Not many people are fortunate enough to meet someone, not to use a cliché, but where they just *know.*

I wasn't taught how to *respect* a woman. How to give generously. I've had to learn that on my own. Now my ideal woman would be someone with a sense of pride and a sense of humor. And deeply spiritual. Because these are the qualities that I look for and that I'm now seeing in myself.

I still know this girl I met when I was thirteen. We're still friends. She's not married, but she has one son that I had the privilege to meet. When I met him, I just couldn't help but think, *Man, that's supposed to be* my *son.* My bond with her is still strong. Cause I can be honest with her, see?—and that's what it's all about, being able to be honest.

I even told her about my condition. Not my addiction, my *condition,* my other thing. My *medical* problem. I have HIV. It was promiscuity, you know? Of course at the time I was drinking and using.

Talking about it makes me remember a time when I was having one-night stands, and as soon as the act was over, I felt disgusted-like. And nine times out of ten, I was high or drunk. Most times I was drinking while that was going on, and that sort of numbed my bad feelings about it. And in the morning when it wore off, I was like, *Damn.* I'd find condoms in my pocket. Ones I didn't use the night before.

I only found out about the HIV in 2011 when I went to prison again, for distribution of cocaine. Upon entering the state prison system they give you a physical, and that turned it up. When I heard the doctor tell me the news, I really couldn't ignore the fact that using was hurting me.

This last time, I was in prison for two and a half years. I was using when I went in, and for a while I was using inside. And I got clean there. I got ten months now.

I'm very much cool with the transformation in me. Now I work on constant spiritual contact. And I take my medication. The advances in treating HIV are just dramatic. See, now, that's hope! That's part of what has me hopeful.

And I believe I'm gonna meet somebody. I'm clean, my mind is focused, my perspective is different. I don't want to just jump in and rush to the act. I'm about that romantic Lifetime Channel type of shit, you know what I mean? Cause that's what I wanted all my life, only I could never admit it to anyone else till I put down the drugs.

That's why I was saying in a meeting the other night that in recovery, my perspective on going out with women is totally different now. My condition puts a whole different spin on it. Because it's now about taking care of me and being responsible. Not getting involved in just any kind of relationship—now I want to be responsible. I don't want to endanger the other person. In *any* way.

I'm really trying now to live a responsible life. I'm trying like hell to get to recovery from this disease and my other illness that came from that. Things like HIV, hep C—we might not have 'em if we hadn't been using, right? So using is the thing that causes that stuff. And we learn in recovery that we live in delusion, so to speak. If we keep on lying to ourselves and other people, we're never gonna be able to change our lives.

So I have a chance now to create a family, and make children who will live this kind of peaceful life I'm livin' now. I can do that if I choose. I can have a peaceful life with a woman.

Recovery to me is to have options and hope. Cause, you know what I'm saying, I don't like to use the term "the hand that you were dealt." That's why I love the whole spiritual aspect of the program. Everybody comes in there with some kind of similar tragic story, shit that Stephen King coulda written, you know what I mean? So to see a person who *comes back* from that hand they were dealt—that's what I *like* about it, you know? I hear a lot of people in meetings who say, "I ain't gonna go through my horror stories," and I'm like, "Man, *please do!* That's what's gonna help me—identifying with you!"

That's the beauty of this other side of life, as I like to put it. I have my spirituality. I have my integrity. I have my peace of mind and serenity. Everything else—it's gravy.

So what I'm talking about is time. Time heals a lot. Everything has its own time, and now's the time for me to work on myself and find myself. And one thing that's said in those rooms is that we're in the right place right now. "We're right where we need to be"—I hear people I respect now sayin' that.

It's good to be talking about this. I mean, I only ever heard of sexuality being brought up briefly in meetings; it's not like we ever talk about it like this, you know, *open.* And you see, this is makin' me think a little! That's a *good* thing.

Honesty and Vulnerability

A woman tells me, in the course of our interview for this book, "My boyfriend and I made love last night." She has four years in recovery. It's her first relationship since she stopped using, and though he's not in recovery, he knows she is. She has been seeing this guy for a little over a year. "And as he touched me, as he put his lips on my body, I had a really tough time being inside myself. It was like I was watching myself from outside my body. I'm getting a little worried because this has been happening off and on for about two months."

She speaks softly and fast, as if she hasn't told anyone else about this. (Later, she says she hasn't.)

I ask her why she thinks she has been having this sexual response, or lack of response. She gives me a bunch of reasons: stress at work, stress at home, fear of personal and professional failure.

"So there I am on his couch and we're making out—he has these really awesome big hands, and while he's kissing me he starts by winding my hair around his fingers, then pretty soon he's got my jeans unbuttoned and he's squeezing my hips. I usually love it when he puts his hands on me, right? But meanwhile, my mind is piled up with all those imaginary disasters. My work will fall through. I won't be able to meet my bills. I'll fail. And underneath everything I always worry that when he squeezes my hips he'll figure out that I'm fat. He's hung around for more than a year, and he says he really likes my body, so how can I be thinking these things?

"I'm not good enough, I'm not sexy enough, I'm not relaxed enough, and pretty soon I start to think the relationship itself will fail. These thoughts occupy my mind. It's like an army in there that has locked me out of my own body. So as he touches me, I seriously can't feel my body."

When they first started dating, she hadn't had sex for two and a half years, and the feeling of his touch was intense. But the longer the relationship continues, the more she feels trapped inside her head.

"It makes me unspeakably sad," she says, "because the more I pay attention to all these worries, the less attention I pay to him. Here's this man, we really like each other, we've hung out together for over a year, and he is *right here*, loving my body. He wants to play. And so do I! But my mind is clogged up with these thoughts, and I get locked out of my body. And I don't know what to do. How can I get back into my body?"

I ask her whether she has ever told him any of these feelings.

"Hell no!" she says. "He'd think I'm nuts. He doesn't need this kind of complicated junk in his life. He'd dump me. I can't imagine trying to talk about feelings with no clothes on without some kind of drug. In my old life, when I knew I was going to have sex, it was so much easier to take a drink or a drug and try to be what I thought the other person wanted me to be than to be honest about my feelings."

How Distortion of the Truth Isolates Us

There are a lot of resources out there that would tell this woman how to have better sex, and I don't just mean *Cosmo*. I mean the PhDs who get paid to study this stuff. Like Emily Nagoski, who might ask the woman to take a Sexual Temperament Questionnaire to find out how strongly the woman's "accelerator" and "brake" are acting on her sexual response. Nagoski might say that the woman's fears of failure put a brake on her response, and that, depending on the questionnaire's results, she might have a slow accelerator to ramp up her desire.[15] Then there's psychotherapist Esther Perel, whose TED talks are about creating space inside a relationship to build desire. She might suggest the woman stay away from her partner for a while to make for a certain level of sexual frustration that creates a *frisson* when the couple finally comes back together.[16] On the other end of the spectrum there's John Gottman, who might tell the woman that her stress has caused a physiological storm called "flooding," which makes her distance herself from her guy, and that the solution to restore connection during sex is for the couple to build closeness and learn to soothe each other.[17]

But none of these researchers—or any others—have studied what happens when addiction enters the picture of sexual response. So again, there's little to no data to go on, but there is a wealth of anecdotal experience. The stories show that when dealing with recovery from addiction, the distortions of truth—the lies and judgments: "I'm fat, I'm ugly, I can't tell the truth because he'll think I'm crazy"—tend to creep into our sexual relationships just as they tend to invade other parts of our lives.

In recovery, we know that when we don't tell ourselves and others the truth, we isolate ourselves. But what we talk about less often, or actually maybe never, is how much harder it is to tell the truth when it has to do with sexuality. Especially when our clothes are on the floor.

One guy I talked with gave a stunning example of the distorted, deluded perceptions during his first sexual relationship in recovery. After quitting drinking and smoking pot about three years ago, he's about eight months into this thing with this woman—whatever it is: "Since I've been hanging with her I've been telling myself that just because I'm having sex with her doesn't mean I'm in a relationship. I tell myself I don't know what to call whatever it is we're doing together. And so I haven't been calling it anything. My friends will say, 'How's your girlfriend?' and I'll say, 'She's not my girlfriend.'

"Then we went on a three-day vacation and we were on the beach talking about how we'd been hanging out for like six months, and she said casually, 'Yeah, we're definitely in a relationship.' As if we'd been in one all along! It seems healthy to me that she could say that so easily, so why couldn't I? I thought about it and I realized that in the first two or three months, after each time I'd see her, I told myself I might never see her again, which is total bullshit, because we were doing awesome, so why *wouldn't* we see each other again?

"I just think that one of the parts of recovery that's so hard and that I have to be so vigilant about is how much these blatant lies can creep into the way I think. Like, I'm telling myself, 'No, I'm not in a relationship,' when actually I *am* in a relationship. I've told myself, 'No, I don't really care that much about her,' when I'm actually in love with her. But have I told her? That's the really hard one: 'Well, okay, I love this person, but I don't actually have to tell her.' Because even though I've dedicated myself to 'rigorous honesty,' she doesn't have to know the truth, right? I don't know what the solution is."

I ask, "Isn't the solution rigorous honesty?"

"I mean I guess so, but that level of honesty is friggin' scary. I don't even really talk about this stuff with my friends or my sponsor. I try to meditate about it, but it doesn't really put a dent in my fear of actually saying my real feelings to this other person."

So there he is, lying next to a woman, I mean lying next to *his girl-friend*, and he has all these feelings dammed up inside him that he cannot begin to express. They could be lying skin-to-skin, but they might as well be in different cities with only smoke signals to communicate.

How often do we say what we truly feel, in or out of the bedroom?

The delusions don't come just from our lack of relationship skills, or our own individual addictions or addictive tendencies, or our inability to rely on a higher power. They also come from an addictive culture that feeds sex-negative ways of thinking. The culture encourages us not to talk to our children about sex, unless we're telling them not to have it. It also veers in the other direction: as girls are trying to attain an impossible ideal of hotness, they're also being fed the virginity story. They're being told to "save themselves," and meanwhile they twerk in the mirror. And both boys and girls gain unrealistic ideas of how they ought to be able to "perform" sexually through the pervasive availability of internet porn.

I told sexologist and addictions counselor Rosalyn Dischiavo that it seemed to me that we were in a sexual straitjacket.

"It's more like a corset," she said. "We're being scrunched in the middle and squeezed toward opposite ends of the spectrum. The people at one end scream at us that there's way too much sex in this culture. But in fact, we do not have too much *sex*—we have too much commercialism. What they're really upset about is the other end of the spectrum: the plethora of sexualized images sold to us from all sides. The idea of sex gets conflated with the idea of what the culture—celebrity culture, the media, consumerism—is selling us, and people get disgusted with that. What we in the public see is this dishonest, materialistic version of sexuality. And we know we're being manipulated and lied to. And we blame 'sex' instead of seeing that it's just a big a sales job."

There's tons of reading out there about how addictive families raise their kids to inhibit or totally ignore their feelings in order to keep the boat from rocking.[18] But what's rarely talked about is how that dishonest family structure affects sexuality—the sexuality of the parents and the ways teenage kids fail to form healthy sexual identities. "One of the rules for the alcoholic family is, *Don't feel. We're already overloaded with unmanageable, unexpressed feelings. We can't afford to have you feel,*" Dischiavo says. "If you're a child of an alcoholic family, god forbid you feel anything strongly.

"But as a human being, one of the strongest things you can feel is sex. If feelings make you vulnerable, then sex makes you even more vulnerable because it means you need somebody, and people with addiction are not good at needing other people."

Samuel, who shares his story in the next chapter, told me the same thing. He's a few months into his first relationship in recovery with a woman who's also in recovery. While drinking and using, he compulsively used porn—and compulsive porn use is not about practicing honesty with another person. After he got sober and started taking his clothes off with his new girlfriend, Samuel discovered all the feelings he'd been hiding in his porn use.

"When I'm sitting here talking about Abby, talking about sex with Abby, I can see our relationship, the whole thing," he says. "I love that woman, and I know she's safe with me. I know that the sex is just a part of what I feel about her.

"But then I have all these questions. Like, let's just say it's a night that we're spending with each other: so how much sex is *too much* sex? When's the right time? What if she's not in the mood for it, and I am: Is it okay to still ask for it? And what if I'm not in the mood and she's coming on to me? When I'm actually *in it*, it's so much harder to be honest. Just like everything else in life, I guess."

So when you combine needing someone with needing to tell them the truth, no wonder the stakes feel so high.

Trying Rigorous Honesty in Bed

Much of American culture still fosters an outdated fallacy from its
Puritan past: we'll grow up virgins, find our one true love, and marry that
person—and we'll never be attracted to anyone else ever again. And we
all know this story is a lie, but many of us try to fit ourselves into that box
anyway. Somehow—possibly with the help of drugs and drinking—we try
to shape our lives according to this fallacy, even when we know it's contrary to our experience. And then we get clean and sober by practicing
rigorous honesty. How can we stay healthy if we can't say the truth about
sex, at least to ourselves?

I talked with a number of people in recovery who were practicing
telling the truth about sex, even while in bed. There was Magdalene, a
sixty-two-year-old woman with twenty-two years of recovery. Her husband is also roughly twenty years clean and sober, and a few years after
they were married, before he got sober, he left her and began dating another woman. Meanwhile, Maggie had been abusing prescription painkillers. "When I was using, all bets were off. I was much more hurtful
to him, because I was hurt by him. We kept hurting each other, back
and forth." But then they both made it into recovery, and after a couple
of years they moved back in together. She had to think carefully about
whether she could let go of her feelings of abandonment and betrayal.

"In the beginning, I was cautious. I was afraid to open up emotionally and be vulnerable again. When he wanted to get back together, I just
thought, 'No way.' I didn't ever want to be hurt like that again. But as time
went on, I realized he was the real deal. His character really did change
when he went into recovery. He was much more present. He wasn't angry
all the time. He wasn't as defensive or volatile. He was able to be much
more honest with his feelings.

"Since we got into recovery, the level of loving each other is the deep-
est change. That has been the greatest gift—love and respect. That goes
for when we're in bed too. I think I have more fun in life now, in every way.
With sex, it's just all part of the rest of life. I still most of the time feel like
I don't have any drive to have sex. But I kind of hop into it, and once I'm
there, I'm okay. I'll say to him, in bed, 'Look, I don't feel like having sex,

but let's just play around and see—I'll get there.' And he understands that not as a rejection of him but as a vulnerability that I'm offering to him so he can love me through that process, and we get to the point where it's fun."

Magdalene worked hard to get to the point where she could be honest between the covers. "First I have to be honest with myself, and then communicate that to him. Making clear that it's not that I don't want to have sex with *him* in particular, but it's just my emotional state that I have to work on at that moment. Before I got sober, it wasn't even like I was too afraid to tell him I didn't want to have sex—it was just that I didn't even *know* what was going on with me. I didn't understand myself. I was hurting myself by not speaking the truth. After getting sober and getting therapy, I was more of a whole person, accepting my flaws more, and knowing I could communicate those flaws, and tell him, 'This really has nothing to do with you, but I want to tell you how I'm feeling.' It seems like a simple thing to say that kind of a sentence, but to me it's huge. I worked many, many years to get to that point."

Different Drugs, Different Effects

While there's some truth to the common notion that "it doesn't matter what you used, how much you used, or where you used," drugs affect the body in different ways. Alcohol, painkillers, and benzos such as Xanax are sedating, and methamphetamine and coke are stimulating. So these different classes of drugs affect sexuality differently. People taking heroin and Vicodin might go months or even years not even thinking about sex. Meth and coke users, on the other hand, have sex compulsively. For example, meth is popular with gay men in certain regions, and guys using meth easily forget to eat or drink water. They may have sex or masturbate so compulsively and so often that their genitals become raw. Gay men and even heterosexuals on meth have more unprotected anal sex than those not on meth.

Aside from the physical risks, meth also wrecks our ability to have empathy, says sex and addictions therapist David Fawcett. The cornerstone of his clients' recovery, he says, is increasing their capacity for intimacy. For meth users, whose receptors may be literally burned out by the drug, he says, regaining sexual desire can take eighteen months of patient, hard recovery work with very little rewards in the form of physical pleasure during that time. He recommends (as do others in the chapter on the One-Year Rule) taking time away from sexuality to focus on our own healing. There's plenty of time after that to work on the kind of honesty it takes for genuine intimacy.

"And by that I mean exploring sex and emotions with one person over time," he said. "Stay consciously present. I mentioned mindfulness before. With meth, it's all a head trip, a fantasy trip. They lose touch with the person in front of them in a deeper way. Stay consciously present. Focus on physical sensations. Try to avoid getting up in your head. . . . Explore giving and receiving."

Sound familiar? Sex educator Emily Nagoski says the same thing: Focus on sensations.

"The ultimate treatment goal for recovery from meth addiction—and I think from any addiction—is mastering the experience of forming enduring and trusting intimate connections," Fawcett said. "And I would add to that, a connection with oneself. It has to start with knowing and believing in yourself."[19]

Cultivating the honesty and vulnerability it takes to form these kinds of connections takes time and patience. It helps to remember that healing from the physical and emotional damage from some drugs, like meth, takes longer than with others—but it can be done.

Experiencing Sacredness

One of the most unsettling and yet oddly comforting pieces of advice that I've ever heard about practicing honesty about sex in recovery came from Gabriel, who tells his story of getting sober in New York City in his thirties. For many years Gabriel, a straight guy who identifies as both Jewish and Buddhist, has practiced Ashtanga, a fairly athletic form of yoga. His practice makes him sweaty and hot, but his primary reason for practicing yoga is not the workout; it's to cultivate awareness of his mind and body. Which is to say, it's to cultivate intimacy with himself first.

"Be really honest," Gabriel said. "Do not take advantage of people in conditions of weakness or vulnerability. Understand that you're giving them something and they're giving you something, and you should treat that as a very, very precious gift. That means even if you're having sex but aren't in a relationship.

"Sex is a big thing to give somebody! It's, like, you know, what giving food meant in the desert, in the conditions of the ancient world. It's something that's very precious and that approaches a sacrament, and we often don't treat it like that, and you don't want to be super pompous about it, but it's like—you're giving somebody *your body*."

. . .

Queries for Discussion

Honesty and Vulnerability

☐ When and how did I first learn about sex? What kinds of attitudes—emotional, physical, religious—did my family of origin show about sexuality? What kinds of judgments did I learn about sex?

☐ Under what circumstances is it easier for me to tell a partner how I feel, and when is it harder? What does "rigorous honesty" mean to me when it comes to talking about feelings with a partner?

☐ What were some occasions when I've had sex against my desire for it? Have I habitually had sex when I didn't want to? If so, what has prevented me from being honest with my partner about this? With myself?

☐ What are the distortions of thought that might prevent me from knowing the truth about what I really feel about sex? What distortions might prevent me from telling my feelings to my partner?

SAMUEL

Giving Up the Secret Fantasies

Thirty-two / Eighteen months in recovery

I'm not saying I was into anything like women getting choked or any of the freaky stuff that's out there. But just like, the fantasy of it: having it the way *I* wanted it, in different positions, and just stuff that maybe my girlfriend might not have wanted to do.

I think it wrecked my ability to appreciate quote-unquote normal, vanilla sex. So-called normal sex didn't give me the same rush as porn. It's hard to describe—maybe it was the lack of intimacy? It didn't have anything to do with what position it was, or what the woman in the video was wearing. It was really just about control. Because depending on what I wanted to feel or see, I could shop around. I could flip to a new video and get that. And I couldn't do that in bed with my girlfriend.

I mean maybe she would have done some of the things that I wanted, but I was too ashamed to ask her.

At that time, a lot of that sex I had, I was drunk and high. And porn was a huge part of my life: just sitting home while my girlfriend, Naomi, was at work or school and masturbating. That was how I passed the time. That was another way of increasing the feeling of not being inside myself and my own body that I was already getting by drinking and using so much.

I was with Naomi for six years, and she broke up with me after my DUI in 2012. The cops arrested me, and I had a blood-alcohol content of over point-three-six, which is more than four times the limit in New York state.

I was in the hospital, detoxing from alcohol and benzos. My dad told Naomi about the trail of money. He and I had a joint credit card and he knew how much money I was spending on booze. And either she didn't know, or she knew and she was in denial.

So there I was in the hospital bed, and my dad was talking to her on the phone. When I woke up, he handed me the phone, and she broke up with me when I was in bed, detoxing.

It was what I needed. I'd never had any consequences until then. The feeling I had was one of relief: I wasn't gonna have to come clean to her about all the lies I'd been living.

My dad talked to me about sex when I was in second or third grade. He used the example of the Discovery Channel—"You know those TV shows about animals? *Mating!* Well, that's what people do too!" And that was the end of the talk. Maybe I blocked out the rest of it, but that's what I took away.

I already knew everything about sex anyway because before that, my cousin, who's a year older than me, introduced me to porn. Back in the nineties, if you flipped up high enough, you could see black-and-white fuzzy porn on certain channels.

So I was in like second grade when I first started watching porn.

And maybe that laid the groundwork for me being obsessed with it later. Because, in my addiction, porn and sex became another way to get high.

When I was sixteen or seventeen, I got my first debit card, and then I didn't have to sneak around my parents, and I discovered online porn. And that became a huge part of my life as a late adolescent and then on through my twenties. That's when I started seriously drinking too.

I first had sex with a real girl when I was eighteen. I was a senior in high school, and she was a junior. We ended up dating for a year and a half. And I thought I was in love, but sex was pretty much the driving factor. I'd get frustrated when I wasn't getting what I wanted, and how much of it, and how often, and in what way. I look at that now through the prism of recovery, and it's just more of the selfish and self-seeking behavior of addiction—it's gotta be the way I want it with everything in my life, including sex.

The other big part of my sex life during my addiction was prostitutes and strip clubs. I must have spent ten thousand dollars over ten years on prostitutes, strip clubs, and porn. I don't bring that up when I tell my story in meetings, except maybe in passing. As soon as I turned twenty-one and I was legal to go to a strip club, I started shopping around.

And then, for prostitutes, there was this one website I'd go to that was known for that. The criminality of it gave me a high. It was the buildup to it more than the act itself that I liked. The actual sex always paled in comparison to what it had been in my head, in like the hour or so beforehand. And from the time I decided to do it, to when I picked up my phone, to when I got my money, got in the car, went to whatever sordid hotel it was, or loft or apartment in the city—that was the thrill of it: getting there, and getting away with it. A lot of it wasn't *sex*. It wasn't as much of a thrill to have *sex* with these strangers. A lot of it was hand jobs, or oral.

My heart was racing as I was parking and going up the steps. Heart was racing when the door was opening. I didn't actually think about the fact that I could get busted and thrown in jail, but still—there was always this fear.

Which was wrapped up in my using too. I was always afraid. But it didn't start out like that in the beginning. Paying for sex was an absolute fear-free rush. It started with the strip clubs, and the rush wasn't about the sex, it was about doing something I shouldn't be doing.

I was involved with Naomi at the time. And that piece was missing: she wasn't sexy enough, she didn't look the right way—pretty basic chauvinistic stuff. I didn't think any woman I was gonna have normal sex with was gonna look like that, and I decided I wanted to—I *needed* to have sex with someone who looked like that. So I'd go shopping.

I kept this a secret from everybody. I didn't tell anybody what I was doing.

In my relationship with Naomi, sex was spontaneous at first, but then it became something that we had to plan. Do you think it winds up that way in all relationships—that you have to plan on doing it?

Then it became something that I had to ask for. I was unhappy in my life, I was drinking more and more, and I also wanted more sex to distract myself from how shitty things were. It was another diversion, another escape.

She didn't feel close to me. We were falling apart. She didn't know how much I was drinking and using, but she could see I was fucked up a lot when she came home. But even if she didn't know fucked up I was, my use of drugs and porn drove us apart. We weren't as close, we were fighting more, and I wasn't contributing to the life we wanted to live.

We grew apart, and we had less sex because of it. Once I started having to ask for it, that felt super shitty. It was one more thing to feel shitty about: "I have to ask for sex." I felt contemptible.

The last time I paid for sex of any kind, I was seven months clean. I wasn't even supposed to *have* any sex the first year in recovery. My sponsor had told me to wait, and I figured it was a question of taking the focus off myself. Like, I shouldn't get entangled in a relationship. So that was another reason that paying for sex seemed convenient. Abstaining from sex took away the risk of entanglement. For the first seven months clean, I didn't have any sex. And that's a long time for a guy thirty years old to wait.

It's really scary to think about that time, because I can see myself going back there. I felt so confident in who I was, with six months or so. And I know now that it was a false confidence. I paid for sex because I came down a little bit off that pink cloud, and I wasn't sure I could wait anymore. And I wasn't willing to go out and meet women with a view toward actual relationships.

Right after that little spree, I had a thing for about a month with a girl I met. Then, when I had almost a year, I had another thing with another girl. But neither of these lasted.

I have eighteen months clean now. For the past three or four months, I've been seeing an amazing woman named Abby.

The sex we have is amazing. And for me, it's true, it's about her body, but it's really about the connection we have. I still think maybe I'm too early in recovery to know for sure whether what we're doing is really intimacy. We're *naked* with somebody—are we being honest yet? Are we actually being vulnerable at that point?

I tell her I love her. She said it to me first, and it was while we were having sex. Yeah, that violates all the *GQ* and *Cosmo* rules, right?—you're not sup-posed to say those words first during sex! But it felt right.

In recovery I've felt all this nervousness and wanting to do everything right. I really want to *do right* by this woman.

I *do* think it's love.

There's a feeling I get when I'm having sex with her. And *face-to-face,* which is not something that I was ever about when I was fucked up. I wanted women in all different positions. And Abby and I have sex like that too. But even better than the sex itself is the intimacy, the face-to-face, and what goes on then—in each other's eyes. When we're looking into each other's eyes, at that point, we're really together.

There's also a little bit of fear in that moment. Eye contact in and of itself is vulnerability. Thoughts race through my head when we're looking into each other's eyes, like, "Am I going to be able to last long enough? Is she gonna be able to come before me?" That's something we should probably talk about more. She tells me not to worry about it. But of course I still worry about it. I don't know why. She hasn't told me it would make sex bad if she didn't come first. We've had experiences where she hasn't come at all, and there's been times that I haven't, and it's been okay, but for some reason that concern has been in my sex life for so long, that voice in my head—that thing where the girl has to have pleasure, I have to get her off first.

Because then there's no risk. Once she's done, I can relax, and I can have more fun.

I mean there's oral, and I can touch her with my hands, and I've done that when I've come first. And that's fine with her. But there's still this, like, *voice.* It's not always a loud voice. Sometimes I can let go and just absolutely enjoy what we're doing, but sometimes that voice makes me feel like I'm not doing enough for her. I'm not good enough.

I feel like I'm overblowing the doubt part of this, because this isn't a huge part of my sex life with her. This is very seldom. But it is there—a quiet whis-per, like, "The *right* way to do it is to satisfy her first."

She doesn't know about my history with porn and prostitutes. She's heard my lead, and I mention this stuff in passing. I'll say, "I spent a lot of money on strippers and prostitutes." That's how I'll frame what I did in my addiction, but she does not know how guilty I feel about what I did a year ago when I was clean.

I haven't even told my sponsor about that yet.

In the beginning, it wasn't necessary to talk about what we wanted. We were so crazy about each other, spending all our time together, and having sex left and right. And also doing everything else in life together.

But we're both really busy, and recently we started having visits where it was just sex. I'd come over for an hour, we'd have sex, and I'd go home. For a little while we didn't talk about it, but eventually we said to each other that neither one of us wants to have the feeling that we're seeing each other just for sex.

At least, not too often. I think it's okay sometimes in a relationship that's strong enough. I think maybe we're worried that we're *not* strong enough. We're just so concerned about doing everything *right.* And that's one thing recovery seems to be doing—it has made us hypercritical of everything we do, including sex.

It helps me to keep cycling. My body—my physical fitness—is one of the areas I'm most confident about in recovery, more so than my motives. It's the one place where I'm like, "Yeah, I'm doing well on this front, for sure, without a doubt." For me, nothing touches the satisfaction of getting on my bike. I got lucky and I stumbled onto my discipline.

I'm getting ready for a race in a couple weeks. Abby and I sometimes ride together. I'm in good shape now, and I never had sex in this kind of physical condition before. And I'm not saying I last for hours—like, this is not some macho thing, okay? I'm not bragging, but it's just like, the workup to it, and the foreplay, and the caressing each other, it can take a long time. Sometimes it goes on for a long time, sometimes it doesn't. But I definitely notice that I have endurance that I didn't have before, just in terms of the positions I can be in, and the things I can do, and how long I can go.

It's funny to talk about these things because I've thought about them, but I've never really put words to them. Talking about this is helping me make a list of things in my head that I want to talk with my girlfriend about.

Clearly, some women turn me on more than others, but I can now see that I just had a real sick view that women were just meat.

Now, I believe everybody's body is beautiful.

Privacy and Secrecy

....

"We're only as sick as our secrets"—so it's often said, as a way to reinforce the imperative that we practice honesty in our lives and recovery communities. Addiction distorts the truth. So if we really want to heal, it's important that we check our perceptions against those of others we trust. It's one way we get healthy.

So does that mean we need to check our perceptions about our sex lives with others in recovery? If "we're only as sick as our secrets," does that mean we'll relapse if we don't reveal every last thing about ourselves?

I wasn't very far into my recovery before I began to wonder how we learn the differences between keeping secrets and having—and even enjoying—privacy. I once asked a friend who's not in recovery how he would identify the difference between these two ideas. (Just the fact that I had to ask him this question makes me feel weird.) "If it's something you've done that you're hiding because you've hurt someone else—that's a secret," he said.

So *hiding* is an important component of secrecy. It's part of addiction's distortion of truth: *I have to hide who I am.* Our sexual education—its poor quality, or the lack of any—begins this process very early. Children are sexually curious from birth, and they naturally explore sexuality starting with their own bodies. How many parents, when their babies or small children's hands wander down between their legs, bat the hands away and tell them it's "bad" to play like that?

Sound familiar?

If I want to have sex just for pleasure, I must be bad.

We have such difficulty staying inside a sensation, choosing instead to judge ourselves. We grow up ashamed of our sexuality, ashamed of our interest in our sexuality, ashamed of pleasure.

But, being human, we explore anyway. So we get used to hiding.

Those of us who grew up in addictive families, with chaos and conflict and almost no privacy, might lack a native understanding of the differences between privacy and hiding, or secrecy.

I sometimes think recovery principles can reinforce the very "defects" from which we're trying to free ourselves. For example, the strong suggestion to check every single perception of mine against that of another person can feed my top shortcoming of approval-seeking: *I can be okay only if you tell me I'm being a good girl (or boy)*. I also often feel forced to second-guess—and third-guess, and fourth-guess—my motives, which makes me trust myself less, not more, and makes me feel afraid of making mistakes.

Making mistakes is, after all, a normal human thing to do. Along with telling the truth, making mistakes is another way we learn and heal. "We all make mistakes" is just as true as "we're only as sick as our secrets"—maybe even more true. To think that we cannot or should not make a mistake, or that our own judgment is something that can never be trusted, can foster self-hatred. And one of the principal purposes of recovery is to learn to trust ourselves.

How Recovery Can Make Us Mistrust Our Judgment

"I'm noticing that we learn to second-guess ourselves a lot," said Shannon, a thirty-five-year-old woman with three years in recovery. "We learn in recovery that we tend to think lies, right? So when you ask me about sexuality, I wonder whether recovery has taught me not to trust myself and what my body tells me.

"For the last nine months, I've been seeing this guy. We have phenomenal sex. It's spontaneous in that we never plan it, but it's also dependable and comforting in that we have sex almost every time we see each other. It's playful and hot without being skeezy or gross. And neither one of us wants to say, 'Is this just sex? Or is it Something More—do we *love* each other?' Because by saying it's just sex, we might trivialize how we feel about each other. But if I were to say I love him, I might flip him out with the subtext that *I just want to get my claws into you.* So I joke about it, or I bring it up in oblique ways. Which is another way of hiding my feelings and keeping secrets.

"For example, are we supposed to call it 'having sex' or 'making love'? In the beginning we called it 'having sex,' but more recently he's started calling it 'making love.' The first time he said that, I joked about it, like, 'Ohhh—so now it's *making love!*' I couldn't risk being serious about it. I couldn't be that vulnerable by saying 'Do you love me?' much less, 'I love you.' Neither of us has said the L-word outside that phrase, but clearly we have really strong feelings for each other. What I'm saying is, we care about each other. I think the quality of love can be measured in terms of the quality of attention two people pay each other, and the attention he pays me, even in bed, is *super high-quality.* I try to give the same kind of attention to him. But despite the fact that I feel like saying 'I love you,' I never say it!

"Like, why can't I say it? This kind of fucks me up, that I can't say something I really feel. One way recovery teaches me to handle stress is to take inventory of what I'm doing. Am I hiding? Am I being dishonest? Or am I just keeping my feelings private so I can see what they are, so I can kind of experiment with them, before I say them out loud?

"There's this message I get in recovery that if I'm not totally exposing myself all the time, I'm not being rigorously honest. Recovery has taught me to question my motives and then cross-examine myself, or even to get other people to cross-examine me: Am I using this person? Am I allowing myself to be used? I go around and around with these daily inventories in the Tenth Step: How have I behaved selfishly today?—well, if I'm having super tons of sexual pleasure with this guy but not telling him I love him when I really do, is that 'self-will run riot'? Is the pleasure that I'm having a lie, or somehow self-involved, just because it's such a great amount? And I ask myself these questions because I've never had a sexual relationship when I was not using. This is my first shot. Since I was eighteen—when I first started being sexual and first started drinking—I have used some kind of drug to deal with getting naked, and I mean naked both physically and emotionally. So as far as being really honest sexually, I'm making all this up as I go along! It's all an experiment. It sometimes feels fun, like playing. I just want to live it all by myself—and if I make a mistake, it'll be my mistake. But other times I feel like I should check *everything* I feel and everything I do against someone else's judgment. Because I often hear people saying, 'I'm an addict, so I'm a liar, and I can convince myself of anything.' And I really don't want to hurt this guy."

Listening to Shannon, I had no answers for her. But I realized she was articulating some problems I'd thought about for a while and had never articulated for myself.

I represented Shannon's questions, anonymously, to Samuel. In the last chapter, Samuel talked about how recovery causes him to question and re-question the quality of his care for his girlfriend.

"I know!" he said, sitting forward. "Is the pleasure *just a good thing?* Can we just *enjoy* each other? Can it just be that simple? Or if it feels that good, is it selfish and addictive? This person just read all my thoughts."

That's when he said, "It's funny to talk about these things because I've thought about them, but I've never really put words to them. Talking about this is helping me make a list of things in my head that I want to talk with my girlfriend about."

So Samuel gives one answer about checking our perceptions against those of someone else: we can check them against those of our partners. It might be just good emotional push-ups for Shannon to get vulnerable and be the first one to say, "I love you." It might also be good for her to wait and keep her feelings private until she's really ready to take that risk.

Fluidity, Body Image, and Self-Acceptance

What does recovery's emphasis on rigorous honesty require of us with regard to being open about our sexual orientation? I spoke with roughly an equal number of men and women for this book, and while I spoke with a number of women who said they were sexually fluid, all the men I talked with said they were either gay or straight. I was unable to find a guy who could talk about sexual fluidity and recovery. I bet I ran into some, but they're not talking about it.

Patty Powers, a New York City–based recovery coach, is adamant in her opinion that men's inability to discuss their sexual fluidity is a risk for a return to active addiction. It's easy for people to imagine and accept the reality of women's fluidity, she said. And we can deal with men being either straight or gay, she said, because we are more ready to accept that people are "born that way."

"But bisexuality implies choice," Powers said, "and bisexual men make people uncomfortable. Very few men tell women about their bisexual past, for fear the women would reject them. What do they do with that past? How do they explore that side of themselves? It's not talked about in magazines, in recovery, anywhere.

"Without people talking about it, how do men who fall into that category express themselves? How can they be honest? If you have this level of confusion and shame around your sexuality and your identity, that could get in the way of your recovery. Men who are truly bi could have a dream of someday marrying a woman and having children. But can they be honest with that woman about their sexuality? It could be a risk.

"I've talked with men who specialize in working with men in recovery and trauma, and they've never thought of it before. It's a really under-researched question."

Powers also raises the question of the ways transgender people are objectified in recovery communities, just as they're objectified in society at large. In the words of Maria Luz, a trans woman who tells her story in this book, "Of course they always want to know what's between my legs." Having worked with so many different people in recovery across the country, Powers has noticed that people "sexualize and fetishize" transgender people. "People wouldn't ask me about my first orgasm on first meeting me, but they do it to trans people all the time," she said. "It's tough, because trans people are finally being heard, but mostly we still treat them as a collection of body parts. Which is a total disservice. If you're talking to trans people in recovery, that's going to be a hot button for them, and you really have to be graceful walking there."

Finally, Powers talked about ways body image impinges on people's sexual identity and comfort. Women, she said, tend to compare their experiences with other women's and judge how they perform in bed.

"I'm talking here, for example, about women who don't like their bodies, who don't feel attractive, who have never had an orgasm, or who have a hard time having an orgasm," she said. "Hearing about women who don't have these problems is a real button-pusher.

"It also affects men who have small penises. It can affect their sexual confidence. But people don't talk about stuff like that. So if you're an addict in recovery, if any of these things are problems for you, and you don't talk about them, it might lead you to seek comfort in drugs."

And looking at these questions honestly, then talking about these questions with others we trust, can give us that comfort. That's changed behavior.

What Is Privacy Good For?

I've given the people who talk in this book ironclad privacy. I promised them that nobody but my editor and I would know their names. I've changed facts about their situations to try to make them unrecognizable. I've also allowed them to read their own contributions to make sure they're comfortable with the level of privacy. Because no matter how much I try to protect their identities, readers will speculate. *Do I know this guy? I bet that's so-and-so.*

Why is it important that I try to protect their privacy?

Because while speculating, readers will also judge. *OMG, that IS so-and-so! Can you believe she did such-and-such?* I am speaking a truth here that we in recovery don't usually speak: We watch each other; we judge each other.

Sex is something our society obscures in privacy. Or does society shroud sex in secrecy? Do we *hide* our sexuality? And if we hide, why do we hide, when sexuality is a generative, healing, pleasurable part of human life?

Yes, we hide. As the stories in this book show, we hide the things we've done that hurt each other and ourselves, and we hide the pleasure we experience with ourselves and others because we learn to be ashamed of feeling pleasure. The stress of the hiding compounds the stress of the harms we've done and the pleasure we experience. For people with certain predispositions—genetic, social—this kind of stress can lead to substance abuse. It can also reinforce and perpetuate the secrets themselves. Physical abuse and substance abuse—perhaps abuse of all kinds— are behaviors that are passed down through generations. And their secrecy is lovingly fostered.

I'm working here to begin to remove the secrecy while maintaining the privacy. It's like picking apart two shirts that have been sewn together, stitch by stitch. It's useless having two shirts sewn together: you can't use either of them. But when they're picked apart, you can choose to wear one or the other—or both, one on top of the other. You can become aware of their distinguishing characteristics and their purposes.

The people in this book are bringing some of their sex lives out of hiding so we can all benefit. If we don't articulate the problems, stresses, and harms, how can we negotiate and amend them? If we don't talk about what the pleasure looks and feels like, how can we play with it and celebrate it as the life-giving force that it is?

The maintenance of privacy, on the other hand, protects their identity. It protects them from judgments and criticisms that are personal. As human beings we form judgments. It's as human a thing to do as to eat or enjoy sex. Studying and practicing the Twelfth Tradition—putting principles above personalities—can tamp down that human urge, but as far as human urges go, nothing ever eradicates them. Whenever two or three are gathered together, there may be a higher power in their midst— sure, fine. And there may also be criticism, surveillance, and that good old middle-school-playgroup bully, Peer Pressure. Which is why it's so important to remember to put love and tolerance first.

Part of loving and tolerating each other is allowing each other privacy. To claim some privacy is to claim two benefits. On the individual level, it lets people experiment, try new practices, and make space to play with identity and grow as a human being without feeling judged. On the group level, it provides for diversity of all kinds, keeping the larger community healthy.[20]

I sometimes think privacy gets short shrift in systems for recovery. Maybe this is because I think of the problem of privacy versus secrecy more as a problem of what we call "codependency"—a failure to form flexible but firm boundaries that allow us to care for others but not at our own expense. Sometimes, we fear addiction's power to distort our perceptions so much that we formulate an idea of recovery as the willingness to disclose everything and anything to at least one person. "My sponsor knows everything about me," we sometimes hear people say (or brag). When I hear people say things like this, I wonder whether they're telling the truth. Is it possible to tell *everything* about oneself to another? Is it even healthy?—especially if, in our families of origin, our privacy was regularly breached and we grew up with constant surveillance?

The Spy and The Judge

It's on our coins and in our literature: *To thine own self be true.* The sweet little slogan comes from Shakespeare's *Hamlet*—it's part of a bunch of advice that Polonius, one of the king's counselors, gives to his son Laertes just before the young man leaves for France. On the surface it's awesome advice, the idea that you must work to trust yourself and uphold your own values. I buy it, actually.

But if you read how it's written in the play, it becomes clear that the father offers this string of advice in a pompous and moralizing way, and later Hamlet pretty accurately calls Polonius a "tedious old fool." Polonius later meets his death by accident while spying on Hamlet, and sex has everything to do with it: Polonius is looking for information about Hamlet's interest in Polonius's daughter, Ophelia. That's right: the tedious old fool dies at the point of Hamlet's sword while violating Hamlet's privacy, conducting surveillance of his sexuality, and assuming the mantle of a judge.

I can speculate all I want, but it's impossible to know the quality of another person's recovery, just as it's impossible to know the quality of other people's relationships or marriages. I can guess till the cows come home, but I'll never know what goes on in someone else's sexual relationship, and I'll never know what goes on in someone else's relationship with their higher power. (Hell, I have trouble enough figuring out what goes on in my own relationships with people and quote-unquote god.) Even if I'm someone's mentor in recovery, it's impossible to know every last thing about that person.

Recovery is not to help someone stay dependent for life on the judgments of others. Here's what recovery is for: to share experience, strength, and hope, and to build a community that supports people with unconditional love, so that they can heal and become spiritually strong enough to trust their own judgment.

* * *

Queries for Discussion

Privacy and Secrecy

☐ How do I understand the differences between secrecy and privacy in my own life? When is it okay for me not to talk about certain feelings, problems, or experiences? When would it be better for me to speak with someone about them? What are the differences between "isolating" and enjoying the pleasure of alone-time?

☐ What did I learn in childhood about sexuality, secrecy, and privacy? Did I learn to hide my sexuality out of shame? What kinds of powers other than myself can I see working in my life to help me replace that shame with acceptance and love?

☐ How can I build flexible but firm boundaries that allow me to share and check my perceptions against others' when I need to, and that don't compel me to overshare when I don't want to?

☐ How can I talk with my children about their need to explore their own bodies and experiment with their own sexuality?

ELAINE

"My Body Is Waking Up"

Twenty-eight / Eleven months in recovery

Until nine weeks ago, I had never had sex while sober. I mean, *ever.*

And I've been having sex for as long as I've been drinking and having my period, basically. So stack up nine weeks of sober sex against *fourteen years* of sex on drugs and alcohol, and there's a lot I have to learn.

The first time in my life that I had sex, I was dating a senior from St. Joe's. I was fourteen. We were drinking vodka in my parents' basement.

He wasn't kind to me. It wasn't anything special. It was like, "Whatever—let's have sex."

At a Jesus summer camp when I was twelve, a girl kissed me in my bunk bed, and I felt like I fell in love with her. I was so enamored. No one had ever paid that much attention to me before. But I was also flipped out. I thought that I didn't know what my sexual orientation even was. Even *thinking* you liked a girl was just so taboo. And of course, there was no one to talk to about it.

So when I was fourteen and this high-school guy started paying attention to me, I just felt like, "Thank god, I like a *guy!*—Let me just do what I'm supposed to." Which meant, basically, "Let me do what he expects me to do."

Like I said, he wasn't kind to me, but I don't remember that night being painful for me. But I mean, nothing about it was right. It was such an unhealthy thing we had. In the first place, no fourteen-year-old should be drinking that much. Or having sex because she thought she was supposed to, because she thought that was what *he* wanted.

And I thought I was supposed to do what *he* wanted.

I don't have any idea of how many people I've slept with. I couldn't even give you a ballpark estimate. I blacked out easily, and I don't even have an idea of *who* I slept with. I don't know how I don't have some kind of horrible disease. I don't know how I wasn't one of those girls who went missing. I was going home with anybody all the time.

I think it started in college. Yeah—five years of sleeping with everybody.

So when I got sober, I didn't know how to clean up the wreckage of what I didn't even know about, what I couldn't even remember.

I talked about it with my sponsor. She never made me feel ashamed. So having those holes in my memory doesn't eat at me. I'm simply grateful that I'm not doing that anymore. My sponsor helped me see the things inside me that led me to that kind of behavior: never liking myself; never feeling I was important enough to come first; always needing to get some kind of attention. Needing to get someone to care about me—or what I thought was someone caring about me. I always needed someone else to make me feel okay about myself, to make me feel like I was pretty enough to go home with.

That was the extent of the meaning of sex while I was drinking and using: *I'm pretty enough to go home with.*

As far as actual relationships, I never had an ordinary relationship. The last ordinary boyfriend I had—before this thing I have now with Caleb—was in high school when I was a senior, and I was also dating a senior. That guy and Caleb are the only two age-appropriate relationships I've ever had. I was always the twenty-year-old dating a thirty-three-year-old, or the twenty-one-year-old dating a thirty-five-year-old.

I've always dated people who I thought I could save. I have this huge savior complex, as if I'm superhuman and can save these guys. I thought if I saved them, they would stay with me. If I gave them enough money, they would stay with me. They were usually with someone else—they had wives, or long-term girlfriends. They usually had children. There was never anything in it for me.

Whatever I had with any of these guys, it was always less about me and how I was feeling and more about what they were feeling. I liked sex well enough, but it wasn't something *for* me. I don't think I was ever doing it for myself. For example, I never masturbated. Like, I never wanted to feel good. It was like I had to make the other person feel good, and then I was allowed to feel good knowing that *he* felt good.

On the surface it was about them feeling good. But underneath, it was really about me knowing that I could make somebody feel good. So it was a manipulation.

So when I got clean and sober, I found out that I actually didn't know what sex was for. I guess I've never thought about it that way before, but that's the truth. I didn't know why people would even have sex.

I was in a relationship when I got sober, about a year ago. The man I was seeing, Tamir, was younger than I was. He was twenty-three, and he had two daughters with another girl, Tyra.

They weren't married, and he wasn't *with* Tyra anymore. But this was typical. I often picked married guys, or guys who had kids with other women. I always wanted them to leave for me, but I never *actually* wanted them to— I just wanted to know that I could make them keep coming to me. There was definitely this competition between Tyra and me. I was with Tamir just so I could make him choose me over his daughters' mother. Another manipulation.

On the last night I ever drank or used, I went over to Tyra's—she lived in the projects—and I got beaten up. She fractured my skull in two places, and she broke my nose and my tailbone.

I have no idea why I went over there. I was in a blackout. I never knew when I'd black out. I'd often black out after sitting down and having one drink—I just wouldn't remember anything else. It was the weirdest thing.

That night, I don't know whether I was drinking really quickly or I was just wasted from the night before. I remember seeing Tamir, and I'm on the ground, and there's a circle of people around me, kicking me. It had turned into a mass of people beating the shit out of me. And then I remember being handcuffed to a hospital bed. I woke up in jail. The cops had charged me with trespass, which is a felony.

So I couldn't see Tamir anymore, obviously.

Within the next month, I was out of jail and finally in recovery. Early on, I gave a lead at a women's meeting at a hospital addiction unit. I was standing there talking to those women, and I realized what had changed for me. I'd had the shit beaten out of me before, I'd been arrested before, I'd been to jail before. I'd gone to jail for public intoxication, and I'd also been arrested for a DUI. So none of that was new.

The reason it was different this last time was that the day I got out of jail, I just knew in my body that something was so wrong. Something inside me was saying, "Being beaten up and arrested is not as bad as it's gonna get."

Three days out of jail I went shopping and I took a pregnancy test in the bathroom. And I was pregnant.

If I'd tried to keep the baby, I would have had to raise it by myself. Or I would have been with Tamir, the father, and I would have been trying to raise the baby always in fear of Tyra.

So I had an abortion. That was what was different. That was what was too much. Because I wanted a baby so badly. I still do. But standing there speaking to those women, I realized I'd gotten into recovery because I finally saw how low my drinking and drugging had taken me. I finally saw what other people had been seeing for so long: this person who was blacking out, having sex with guys who didn't care about her, putting herself in situations that were life-threatening, getting pregnant when she wasn't able to support a baby—that was not who I really was. I was in a pitiful state. I finally saw that recovery had to come first.

It took me about a month to have the abortion. I was in outpatient treatment at the time, which was good because it was a safe place for me to spend the day and cry.

Tyra and I were going to court back and forth. She was pressing charges. I had blocked Tamir's phone number, so for a long time I didn't talk to him. And then eventually I told him I'd had the abortion. At that point, I was such a different person. I was sober and didn't have any interest in talking with him, much less being with him.

Nine months of sobriety was very hard for me, because I knew I'd gotten pregnant right around the time I got into recovery. I knew I would have been having a baby at that moment. That was just two months ago.

How did I deal with that grief? I have a good friend in the program who's a few years older than I am, and she had been raped. And she just happens to be a trauma counselor. At the same time I was in grief about getting pregnant and having an abortion, she was in grief about being raped. And even though we were grieving about different things, her one-year anniversary of the rape came up, and the nine months came up for me at the same time. We understood each other. There were feelings I couldn't even describe that she just understood.

Meanwhile, I met Caleb.

He and I waited before we had sex.

I mean we didn't wait *that* long, but we waited a few months. Like, two and a half.

We just took walks and hung out. We went on bike rides and on real dates. So by the time we had sex, I knew him, and he knew me. He saw things I don't like about myself, and he was okay with them. I knew he didn't judge me. I knew he was planning on sticking around, at least for a little bit. I knew that sex was not the only thing he wanted from me. I knew he wasn't just going to screw me and then take off.

He kept going on dates with me and talking with me. And he didn't judge me or leave. Which was definitely weird for me.

When we first had sex, it was scary on a lot of different levels. I'm on birth control, but now I'm always scared that I'll get pregnant. And at first, I was so scared that it was hard for me to let go, to just be comfortable with him and have pleasure. But that didn't last for long because he shows me how much he cares about me. I can tell that he appreciates me. So that made it easier to become comfortable with him and his body.

I'm also always scared of whether it's real or not. I still have a hard time believing he could like me as much as he says he does. He treats me so well, and he's so kind to me, and honest with me, that the sex—the actual physical part of it—feels *sooo* amazing. And then later in the day we can go for a bike ride, and get ice cream, and laugh like we're best friends. So, I mean—is that *real*? Can you *have* all of that?

Because I never did before.

It's so cool that I can be connected so deeply with someone. It's almost like there are these invisible threads that connect us even when we're not together.

At first, it was terrifying. I didn't want him to *get* me like that. I didn't want him to know when I was feeling weak, because I didn't want him to use that against me. And since he knows me really well now, he knows things about me before I tell him, so now I can't control what he knows.

So all the manipulation is off the table now. It's gone! And that was so scary.

But now it's more of a blessing than anything.

I think it scares Caleb a lot more than it scares me, the weird connection we have when we're not together. It terrifies him. I think he hasn't been cared about that much or that deeply. I'm just naturally more okay with it. I don't want to figure it out. I just want to accept it. But I think he wants to figure it out—he wants an explanation.

Sometimes it's getting to be annoying. Sometimes I just want to be able to be upset, let it pass, and move on without these sensors he has that make him understand that I'm upset.

I didn't know what sex was for when I first got sober, but I'm starting to get an idea. Right now, it's a way for me to feel much closer to him. It's a way for me to show him how much I care about him, and for me to feel that back.

On a very primitive level, it's just a way to feel so good. Which is such a treat, oh my god!—it's *amazing*.

I also think it's something that we do that nobody else does with us, and that's cool, because we share a lot, we do things with lots of other people, but sex is something just for us. And I like that! I've never felt that before.

I feel like my sexuality and my body are waking up. But it's a little different for me—I feel like I've already *been* with everyone. So now my body is waking up and it wants to have something special. It wants not to be taken for granted. It wants not to get into fights.

I had never had sex without drugs before I had sex with Caleb. And at first it was scary. But it was special, and it felt right.

Consequences

. . . .

Here's a personal story about sexual consequences of addiction. Six months into using heavy opioids for pain, I began to notice that I was losing control of my use—one of the signs that addiction is setting in. Another year passed, and I noticed that I hadn't had a period in those twelve months. I was in my mid-thirties, and it's not good for a woman that young not to be having a period. Conventional medical opinion says lack of estrogen can make bones much more likely to break—for example, when you fall off your bike. Which happened to me. I fell off my bike, and I dislocated and fractured my elbow.

When I told my doctor I wasn't having periods, she ordered a bone-density test, which showed that in my late thirties I basically had the bones of an eighty-year-old woman.

So what did the doctor do?

One thing she did not do was to say, "These drugs are taking away your sex hormones, and you need your sex hormones. Plus, I think you have addiction because every time you come in here your heart is racing and you're sweating like a pig in a barber shop." Instead, she switched painkillers. The medical model is devoted to drugs as a solution to problems. And in some cases drugs can be helpful. But in this case, they weren't.

Of course, being in my active illness, which distorts the truth, I didn't draw her attention to the fact that I had this other problem: *Hey, I'm coming down with addiction!* She would have kicked me into the psych ward.

So with both of us ignoring certain truths in this medical situation, what the doctor did was, she switched me from morphine to fentanyl.

Fentanyl is the strongest opioid made. Most people don't know this, because heroin has the reputation as the world's most badass opioid: *Most addictive drug on the planet, you take it once and you're addicted*, which is garbage, but still, that's heroin's rep. In comparison to heroin and morphine, which are roughly equivalent in strength, fentanyl is by most estimates about eighty times stronger. (A fun fact that the doctor had never told me, even when she first started giving me free fentanyl lollipops to add to the morphine.) Heroin that's laced with fentanyl is a lot more deadly than plain Mexican brown.

Another fact the doctor did not tell me, and that I failed to research myself, was that there are important differences in the way morphine and fentanyl behave in the body. Perhaps the most critical one is their solubility in either water or fat. Morphine (like heroin) is water-soluble, so it has a harder time getting to the brain than fentanyl, which dissolves very quickly in fat. Morphine is a dirty old diesel bus; fentanyl zips into the brain like a clean, quiet, hybrid express train.[21]

Somehow, once my body had gotten rid of the morphine I'd been taking for years and was only processing fentanyl, my period came back, though it was weird—erratic and heavy. But the fact that I even had a period proved that my body was producing at least some sex hormones. In the doctor's mind, this would protect me from osteoporosis. The switch "worked." She kept me on the fentanyl.

But in that time, the other problem—my addiction—continued to progress. Once I was on this exceptionally strong drug that penetrated my fat cells and saturated my liver and brain, I had no idea how to get off. I seriously thought I might be on fentanyl for the rest of my life. I ran out a couple times, and the withdrawal was apocalyptic—much worse than with any other drug I'd taken.

Why is this a story of the *sexual* consequences of addiction? Because when morphine shut down my endocrine system, I couldn't feel that tiger cub clawing inside my belly, saying, "It's sexy time! Let's go crawl up next to our partner and purr!" That tiger in the belly is the built-in sexual response of the human animal. For many women it may rise and fall with factors such as fluctuations in our hormones. In either men or women, when drugs suppress these hormones, the tiger goes to sleep. If we take drugs for long enough, the cat hibernates.

This doesn't happen only to women. Liam, a thirty-year-old man, told me heroin killed his sexual response. Those who have abused heroin or prescription painkillers or who have taken Suboxone or methadone in high doses might recognize themselves in his story.

"One night I went and got a bundle of heroin," Liam told me. "I went to a concert at the Oracle in Oakland, and I was meeting some people. This one girl showed up from LA: she was visiting a friend of mine. I had all these drugs I was gonna do. But she was attractive and I thought, 'I haven't had sex in a while—maybe I *ought* to have sex tonight. But I have this heroin. So I have to choose. Because I want to do this heroin really badly, but then I won't be able to perform.' So I did some of the heroin, enough to satisfy the need, and then I remember going out with her. We danced and drank, and I went back home and slept with her. And *the minute* I was done sleeping with her I went and banged the rest of the heroin. Eventually, in my heroin use, I didn't even look for sex anymore. I just went for the drugs."

Think about his decision-making inside addiction: he looks at an attractive young woman and thinks, *Maybe I ought to have sex now because I haven't had it in a long time.* This is not a guy who is in touch with his sexual response. It's a guy who's looking at the two different drugs on offer.

"Then I got sober," he said, "and my libido came back like a dam breaking. I mean it was so strong with me that while I was in withdrawal I had spontaneous orgasms."

It's not just heroin and painkillers that deaden our libidos. It also happens with booze, benzos, sleeping pills and other sedatives, and Suboxone and methadone—opioids that are used rarely as painkillers; most often they're medication-assisted therapy for opioid addiction. Many people have written to me over the years asking, for example, "I've been taking sixteen milligrams of Suboxone per day for six years—why do I no longer care about sex?" This is why.

For most of us, one consequence of substance abuse is that we no longer experience our real sexual response, whatever that may be. Many people who abuse stimulants (Adderall and other ADD medications; cocaine and crack; methamphetamines) want to have lots of sex, too often, for too long, and too roughly, because these chemicals stimulate the central nervous system and drive up the production of dopamine. Numbing out the human sexual response and putting it into overdrive are just two sides of the same coin: in either case, we don't know how we really feel. When we numb out or otherwise use drugs that fiddle with our sex hormones, it can create problems in our sexual relationships—with others, and especially with ourselves.

After we detox, as Liam's story illustrates, our bodies swing in the opposite direction for a while, then they try to find out what's normal for us. And what's normal might be a pleasant surprise.

Sarah Hepola, author of the memoir *Blackout,* said she had hardly ever had sex without alcohol. "Part of why I drank was to make myself feel sexier. If you took the alcohol away, I hated myself so much," she told me. And after she got sober, she stayed away from sex for two years, partly because having sex without booze was just unimaginable to her. "When I was drinking, I remember thinking, 'Blow jobs are no big deal,'" she said. "When I got sober, I was like, *Oh my god, that's so intimate. There's gonna be a penis in my mouth?*"

Eventually she learned how to find out what she liked, and then how to say it. "You know that last scene of the film *Don Jon*—the whiteout of Joseph Gordon-Levitt having sex with Julianne Moore?" she asked me.

"Yeah," I said. "She tells him that the whole point of sex is to lose yourself not in porn's fake images of body parts, but in another person who's real and right in front of you."

"Right!" she said. "It's a blissfully erotic scene and it reminds me of times after I got sober, when I'd have sex with somebody I trusted and felt connected to. There was this whole wash of dopamine. I'd lose myself. It would be so incredible. I was like, 'Oh—this happened when you were not drinking!' You get the effects of drinking without drinking. That's why the attraction is called *chemistry.*"

For me, the ability to feel that tiger cub tumbling around in my belly is a connection with a power greater than myself. You can call it chemistry, or the innate human urge toward health, or Gaia, Devi, Shakti, or Iron John. If we numb the pain, we're going to numb the power for pleasure as well.

Addiction, Recovery, and Unprotected Sex

Recovery systems that aim for abstinence tend to focus on the spiritual damage of addiction, but the physical consequences can be equally dire. They can affect our sexuality, and we may have to live with some of these consequences for the rest of our lives. Maria Luz, for example, tells a story in this book of riding the merry-go-round of drinking and using. She sold her body so she could drink and use; then she drank and used in order to get into those back seats and sell her body. While trapped on that carousel, she came down not only with addiction but also with HIV, and she has to live with both these life-threatening illnesses for the rest of her life. HIV exposure is one serious result of substance abuse, and it makes it a hell of a lot harder for Maria Luz to start new sexual relationships. There is no easy solution to this consequence for anyone who sustains it. For Maria Luz, finding peace of mind about this physical consequence is a matter of bringing her spiritual principles to bear on her sexual relationships in conscious ways. "I've been positive now for over nineteen years. My health is good. I'm physically well," she told me. "HIV is no longer an automatic death sentence, but some people are still ignorant about that. When I date, though, I have to tell the person that I have HIV. Sometimes I've been rejected because of it."

In addition, if we ignore our sexuality as a component of recovery, we're prone to acting out and making mistakes that hurt ourselves and others. I talked with a number of people who had first had sex in unsafe ways not in active addiction, but in recovery. Joseph—whose story follows—is just one example. And Dré tells of discovering when he got sober that his years of promiscuous sex and paying for sex, while too wasted to use a condom, resulted in HIV exposure.

There are other reasons why people might have unprotected sex inside recovery. The fact that we can "get the effects of drinking without drinking," as Sarah Hepola said, can scare some recovering people into thinking sex might really be a drug. Their response to this fear might be to try to pretend every sexual contact is a relationship. "Often, women in recovery become serial monogamists in very short-term relationships, having unprotected sex with a stranger they've known for a week," says Patty Powers, a New York City–based sober coach. "They can't allow themselves to have sex just to satisfy their sexual desire because they'd judge themselves as a slut. I tell people that having unprotected sex in any situation is a suicidal tendency. It's a choice toward self-hatred and worthlessness. It goes against everything we're trying to do in recovery." Which is not just to stay alive, but to live with self-respect and an improving quality of life.

Thirteenth-Stepping

Then there's "Thirteenth-Stepping," a situation in which people in early recovery fall headlong into a sexual relationship without really knowing what they're doing. Usually one person has a lot more recovery time than the other; sometimes that person preys upon the newcomer's vulnerability.

I've heard of maybe one or two Thirteenth-Stepping stories that have ended in marriage—even good marriage—but most often the stories I've heard had painful consequences. While interviewing for this book, I was in the unexpected and rather unenviable position of speaking with both people involved in a Thirteenth-Stepping situation. I didn't know I was talking to both sides until I showed up for the second interview and it became clear. What could I say? I sat down and listened. The man had many years in recovery and was much older than the woman; the woman was a newcomer, in and out, struggling to put together clean time. She had also been diagnosed with two psychiatric disorders.

As I compared what they told me, it was a case of "he-said, she-said."

He said he'd told her he was sterile. He told me he believes he is. So he did not insist on using a condom, despite the fact that either of them could also have been carrying illnesses.

She said when he told her he was sterile, she didn't believe him—but she still didn't use a condom. Plus, while she was having sex with this guy, she told me she was also meeting other men on Tinder. With one of these hookups, the condom broke, and she took a morning-after pill.

"So at this point, I don't really know who the father is," she told me. "I'm seven months pregnant. I was in a relapse, and I was being very promiscuous." This whole situation seemed to me an example of why the age-old One-Year Rule has been passed down through the generations.

It's hard to ask a seven-months-pregnant woman why she didn't have an abortion. But given the circumstances, the question seemed as if it were sitting on the table between us, so I asked it. And I loved her answer. It wasn't about how the baby would "save" her or how abortion would destroy the baby. It was about how if she'd chosen abortion she might have destroyed herself. "I just know how I am," she said quickly. So quickly that it was clear she had given the question much thought. "I'm so good at finding things to be hard on myself for, and I probably would not survive if I was to have an abortion. I'm all for it—if it's your choice, do it. But I knew personally that I would never be able to stay sober if I had one."

It didn't seem to me that this woman had been preyed upon. She seemed fairly conscious of her behavior and understood that she was now dealing with the consequences of her own choices. But this is not always the case. As a middle-aged woman with six years of recovery, it has appalled me to listen to a twenty-something woman with, say, six weeks talk about how a particular man sits next to her every single time she shows up at a certain meeting, puts a hand on her arm, whispers in her ear, offers to "help" her in her recovery, and then tries to get her phone number afterward. The power balance between genders is so unequal in our society, and the denial inherent in addiction is so persistent, that the guy might not even be conscious of his own manipulation, however many years of abstinence he has.

We ought to get rid of the term "Thirteenth-Stepping" because it minimizes the real problem of people exploiting recovery communities for sexual opportunity. However common or rare it may be from region to region or city to city, it's best to call this what it is: sexual harassment, characterized by a power imbalance used to manipulate someone more vulnerable. The phrase "Thirteenth-Stepping" essentially assumes harassing vulnerable people is a normal extension of the steps we take toward health and well-being. Whether or not Twelve Step fellowships decide to take more of a role in preventing such conduct, the fact remains that the very existence of sexual harassment and its coy name of "Thirteenth-Stepping" result from our society's inability to engage in or tolerate frank, honest discussion and education about sexuality. Because drugs of all kinds are so prevalent in our society, I think Twelve Step recovery is one of the great countercultural movements of our time. And, in line with all the other countercultural attitudes taken by people in recovery, we need to understand that it's up to each of us to govern our own sexual responses and to look after those who are more vulnerable than we are.

Judging Ourselves and Others

As I tell the story of these real people grappling with problems we hardly ever talk about, I have two thoughts. First, I wonder whether we could prevent situations like sex during blackouts, HIV exposure, and unexpected pregnancy in early recovery if we as a society were able and willing to foster more honest public discourse about sexuality.

And second, I'm worried that I'm inviting readers to judge these people.

Anybody who doesn't use a condom is just asking for it.

She made her bed, now she has to lie in it.

I want to say, "You know what, her dad kicked her around so hard when she was little that he went to jail for it. I don't judge her because she wants to have somebody's arms around her now and then."

The society at large seems to expect men to satisfy their horniness with casual sex, while it judges women who do the same thing as "sluts." Sexual contact with recovery newcomers is usually spoken of in either joking or abhorrent terms if it's spoken of at all, while the more common shroud of silence around it permits it to go on. I know and love people who have engaged in it, and I've even secretly judged them myself, despite my love for them.

This is me being honest, here. I can imagine the thoughts running through some readers' minds, because they've run through my own: *He had all those years of recovery behind him, and there he was, putting the moves on a newcomer.* Those judgments say more about me and my own frailty and self-censure than they do about the people at whom they're directed.

The fact is, it's none of my business who sleeps with whom.

But it's also a fact that we're human beings: we judge. Not only that, it's all but impossible to get rid of our judgments—they're inscribed in our consciousness from a lifetime of consuming what our parents, families, schools, the culture all serve up. What we can do is become aware of our judgments, admit them, then inquire into them as a way of changing them.

The Big Book provides the model on which Twelve Step recovery systems are built, and despite its brevity, the Big Book's section about sex is one of the most helpful parts of the sacrosanct first one hundred and sixty-four pages, mostly because it sets up a complete refusal to pass judgment on anyone for anything regarding sex. And like anything made by any human being, it doesn't always succeed. The Big Book was written in the 1930s, and its language and attitudes are a product of its times. Get this passage: "We realize that some people are as fanatical about sex as others are loose." We no long call people sexually "loose," right? But we still call people "whores," "bitches," and "sluts." We call people "players." Either aloud, or to ourselves.

One of the things I like best about these five hundred and seventy-eight words is that they work toward accepting the fact that it's part of the common human experience to struggle at least sometimes in discerning the right thing to do in sexual situations. "We want to stay out of this controversy," it says. "We do not want to be the arbiter of anyone's sex conduct." It mentions that we're born with "sex powers," which must mean they can be used for our own and others' good. And it asks us to write a sex inventory and to shape a "sex ideal" for the future.

"Sex ideal"? This phrase was confusing to some of the people I spoke with. Some of the men seemed to think it encouraged them to imagine their ideal partner. Most of the rest of the folks I talked to interpreted it to mean the principles that guide our conduct. The sex ideal that can be most helpful in the beginning is simply the willingness to change our own attitudes about sexuality—to investigate the personal qualities that drove us in our own sexual history, to identify patterns of helping and harming, and to change the harmful behaviors, which is the nature of amends. And that's the final chapter in our topics series.

. . .

Queries for Discussion

Consequences

☐ In what sexual situations have I been tempted to have, or have I actually had, unsafe sex? What were my motives? In what ways was I being dishonest with myself and with my partner?

☐ In what ways have I pretended about my motives, rather than being honest and looking at the truth?

☐ What self-judgments or critical attitudes might prevent me from getting my sexual needs met in consensual ways when I'm not in a committed relationship? In what ways do I allow myself to take care of my own sexual needs? In what ways do I prohibit myself from caring for this part of myself?

☐ What are my sexual values and ideals? What are the principles that guide me in deciding whether, when, and how to be sexual?

JOSEPH

Finding Sex That's Healthy and Exciting

Fifty / Fifteen years in recovery

During my first month of high school we had a dance, and I knew I couldn't show up to the dance sober. So I went to my brother, who I hated because he was a drug addict, and I asked him to teach me to smoke pot.

Before the dance I went to the cemetery and drank and smoked pot the way he taught me, and I showed up at the dance drunk and stoned and kind of spinning, and then I left, went home, and passed out.

In high school I drank once in a while, but it wasn't until I went to college that I started drinking more regularly. I would go out to a bar and come back and study drunk.

When I was earning my PhD, it was different. That was an eighty-hour-a-week commitment. I couldn't use every day when I was working like that.

So when I got my degree and I moved to New Orleans, I felt like had so much free time that I went out to the bar every night.

When I quit booze and coke fifteen years ago, I had been with my lover Michael for a little over six years. When I quit, he cut back and drank like a normal person. What I didn't know was that he was a coke and pill addict. He worked as the day manager of a gay bar. He'd drink in the morning and switch to pills and coke in the afternoon. He wasn't *drunk* when he came home, but he was fucked up.

He had AIDS, and he was in the hospital often. One day in the hospital he asked me to get something out of his bag. You know what I found?– marijuana, cocaine, Vicodin, sleeping pills, Percocet. The whole shebang. He had tried quitting coke, and he was going through withdrawal. To take the edge off, he was taking all these drugs. He overdosed in the hospital. And my sponsor at the time was the charge nurse at that hospital, which was so cool. I'd go to his office for an hour and he'd calm me down and send me to a meeting.

I went back and told Michael, "You know, this recovery thing is working out for me pretty well." I was four months sober. My life got better really fast. I mean, *really* fast. Life got so much simpler.

It made me aware that my relationship was complicated. We were already in couples therapy. The way couples therapy works is that each individual works on their own behavior. And I was in this program of recovery, but there was Michael, still doing the same stuff. I had gotten sober March 10th, so I told him, "You have till next March." My sponsor had told me not to make any changes for a year.

He tried to quit. He tried Cocaine Anonymous; he tried this and that. He said he was sober and going to meetings.

I had a big party planned for his birthday in mid-November. I went into the top drawer of our dresser to find a bow tie and came across a baggie of cocaine with a silver-plated pen cap. I went through with the birthday party, but afterward I said, "You know, Michael, this isn't working out."

New Year's weekend he cancelled every one of our plans. He found an excuse to go to work every day. I knew he was using. I had enough sobriety not to call him on it. New Year's Day I got a call from his coworkers to pick him up because he was so fucked up that they didn't want him to drive, and I said no.

The day after that I asked him to move out.

I think the most powerful principle of the program is honesty. And it's on the back of the chip: *To thine own self be true.* If I can't tell the truth, and be true to myself, I fracture my entire spiritual being. The deceit will disrupt every part of my life.

So once I had that insight, I *couldn't* live with that behavior. That led me through surrender to acceptance. I grieved. But I had to go through it. And so it wasn't about "How do I *feel* about the end of this relationship?"—I was sad, yeah. But I felt like I was executing a command. There wasn't a choice. There was no going back and reversing this.

Two weeks later Michael went into rehab after living with his mother and hitting rock bottom. Three weeks into rehab I still hadn't spoken to him. I'd made the decision that I didn't want to get back with him—that after two years of therapy and seeing what he'd gone through, I just didn't see us together anymore. I couldn't let him come home thinking that everything was fine. And he was supposed to get discharged on Mardi Gras weekend. I asked myself, was I going to let him come home and tell him over Mardi Gras that I was breaking up with him?

So I broke up with him in rehab. I wanted him to be in a safe space. He ended up staying an extra week.

We're best friends now. We're like brothers. He's been clean for fourteen years. He doesn't go to meetings. He suffers greatly from depression and anxiety, because he has no tools to help him cope with life. I realize that the program is not for everybody—some people are able to stay sober without it. But Michael is so unhappy.

I think those of us with addiction have pain in our lives that fuels this illness. It could be childhood trauma, sexual abuse, or getting picked on. Many of us have this extreme pain that drives us to numb that pain. And the only way we can get sober is when the pain of addiction is greater than the pain of the trauma.

I have friends who have been through childhood sexual abuse, and they can't bring themselves to go through the Steps because they've built up these walls against looking at the truth. So they hit bottom over and over and over, and some of them quite literally.

Specifically I can say many of the gay men I know over forty suffer from PTSD. Let's turn the tables for a minute. So if you're a straight woman, imagine you're a little girl growing up, learning about love. Your parents are two women, and they tell you that one day you'll grow up to marry a woman. And that if you ever think about being attracted to a man, you are evil, you'll go to hell, you're sick.

And these attitudes get reinforced by what you're taught in school, what you're taught by your government, and what you see in the media. All those things tell you that your natural inclinations are wrong, sick, and evil.

If a lesbian couple raised a straight child like that today? They'd be arrested for child abuse. Because they have tormented this child and threatened this child with unspeakable things—fire, brimstone, damnation, being ostracized from the community. Conditional love. This is all mental torture.

How many children have been raised with these twisted views of their own sexuality? With these twisted ideas of what love means?

So how does a gay man deal with a history like this?

The gay man craves acceptance and connection. *Craves* it. And we crave the need to prove we're not bad people. We get the feeling of acceptance and connection through sex. But we might also feel worse, if we grew up with religious or social rules telling us sex is bad, and gay sex is *evil.* Many gay men acquire things to prove they're good. Things: cars, furnishings, clothes. And relationships.

I learned I had to try to create this *image* of being better than everyone else. Because if it *looks* that way, it must *be* that way, right? I have a nice house, a nice car, I look good. I can pass for actually feeling good in my life. I can pass for *being good.*

What's really refreshing is, I don't see the young gay men doing this. I would like to know whether they use at the same rates we did. That would be an interesting study to do. I bet the answer is that the rate is lower now.

After breaking up with Michael, I went through a period when I wanted so badly to have a boyfriend. I was still early in recovery, and I had just lost this long-term relationship. I began to date this guy, and I had it in my head that if he was willing to have unprotected sex with me it implied a commitment. I did this after *twenty years* of having safe sex. I knew that I was HIV negative, and he told me he was. He said he believed he was.

We're both positive now. Eventually he came into recovery, and now we're friends. We're good friends, actually. We co-hosted a dinner party a month ago. We're able to do things that good friends do.

But I very consciously fooled myself that if we had unsafe sex—if we were mutually endangering ourselves and each other—it implied a commitment. It was the idea that in order to have sex I had to have *commitment* that led me to endanger myself like this. I thought, "If he's committed to me, then anything we do must be okay."

And the first time we had unprotected sex, I just *knew.* Maybe it was just the shock of the first time in twenty years of having unprotected sex. It was a *shock.* The fact is, when you have protected sex, all the semen goes into the condom, right? And when you don't use a condom, well—where does it all go? It was such an unusual feeling, the come needing to come out.

Right away I thought, "Did I just expose myself?"

Later, I was going to the doctor for something else. He asked, "Is there any reason for me to test you for HIV?" I had always said no. But this time I said, "Well, yeah, there is." So then I get a phone call on a Friday from the nurse who said the doctor wanted to talk about my test results. I knew that meant I was positive.

That weekend, I went to the New Orleans Roundup—the gay-and-lesbian recovery conference. I met this really nice guy from Dallas. He kinda fell for me and I kinda fell for him. We didn't have sex. But on the Monday after I'd gotten the test results, he called me, and I talked with him about it. It was just such a wonderful gift that he stayed on the phone with me and listened.

I don't believe God manipulates my life. What I believe is this: because I didn't stay locked in my house, because I went to the roundup anyway, even after I knew I was HIV positive, I was able to find this stranger who helped me get over this really heavy news. But also as soon as I found out about my HIV, I went to a meeting and shared the news. I went to thirty meetings in thirty days and shared about it at every meeting. I learned that I can't have any secrets in my recovery program. If there's something I can't tell my home group, then I need to find another home group.

I felt like the people in those meetings were physically holding me up, almost as if they were literally lifting my body up. People shared how good it is to bring heavy news to a meeting. They didn't talk about my health status; they talked about what a good process it is to be able to share intimately with a group of people who really care about you, and to use the program to work through those traumatic events in our lives. And by working on our well-being, we continue to do the next right thing.

Even though we don't *feel* good we can continue to *do* good.

I had to write a Fourth Step. I had to look at my part in this. I had to learn from that. I learned that if I had admitted to myself that I just needed someone to hold me through this difficult time after ending my long-term relationship, then I would have been honest with myself, and that honesty would have enabled me to be honest with this other guy, and I would have protected myself.

In a larger sense, I learned that after I broke up with Michael I was trying to control my life too much, trying to lock away my feelings of grief, trying to force a committed relationship to happen to make myself feel more secure in my life.

I learned I was desperate for love as something outside myself to fix myself. And trying to exert my will over the vast majority of life that I can't control.

There's another problem I have. For me, sex within a loving relationship becomes boring very fast. When I was with Michael, within a couple years I lost sexual attraction to him completely. By the end, it felt almost incestuous, as if I were having sex with a brother.

I was married for four years, and it ended three years ago. In my marriage, we had sex periodically, but again, after a couple years it felt awkward.

We talked about it. He said he was okay with the awkwardness, that he loved me so much that he was willing to stay. But after I found out he was having an affair, I realized the truth: the attraction had dissipated, and I couldn't pretend it wasn't a problem.

So that leads me to the question: Why would I want to have sex with someone I love and respect? I mean, if it's just going to become boring, then why?

Somehow I have it in my mind that sex is supposed to be mysterious, maybe secret, maybe taboo. In fact during puberty, that's what sex was. I had to hide any sexual behavior, and so actually *having* sex became super titillating, an enormous rush.

I don't think I've ever been able to unlearn that way of thinking about sex.

So in recovery we can say that "just having sex" is okay. And it can be okay having one-night stands, or sex only for the sake of sex. But what if, for me, "just having sex" means having sex that is adventurous and exotic and dangerous? What if it means anonymous sex—like inviting a stranger to my house, and he could have a gun? So by continuing to have sex that has this edge to it, am I reinforcing my sexual stereotype, and therefore taking myself further away from romantic sex, or sex inside a relationship? Am I hurting myself by having this kind of sex, and if I am, how do I find my way toward having sex that's healthy and that stays exciting and fulfilling?

We can say that it's okay to have hookups to satisfy sexual desires. The easy answer to the question of whether it's okay to have hookups is yes. But the longer answer is, it might be screwing up my ability to have sex within the context of a loving relationship. When sex is safe, comfortable, and loving, but my sexuality was formed at a time when sex was the opposite of those things—then how do I function in a new way?

I've gone through therapy for a long time to try to answer these questions. Unfortunately, to work through them, I kind of have to be in a relationship with someone. To explore healthy sex—how can you do that without a relationship?

I continue to try to work on answering these questions. I wrote a Fourth Step on my marriage. It became very clear that I have a pattern of choosing people who are in some kind of big life transition, because they become dependent on me and more easily give me the power to make decisions.

For example, my husband was in nursing school, so I was paying all the bills. To me, that seemed very normal, and we loved each other, and I always assumed that one day he'd return the favor. Also, if I'm in love with someone, I'm not gonna go on vacation and leave him home, or go to nice restaurants and not bring him with me. On a conscious level, everything seemed normal and natural and reasonable.

But why did I pick a guy in the middle of a big transition in the first place?

If I were to start a relationship with someone with a stable job and a stable home—if we were to combine our households, that would raise all kinds of questions that are threatening to me because I can't control them. Would I have to sell my house? Would I have to move for this other person? How much of my life would I have to change? By choosing people who have less power in their lives, I can avoid facing these questions.

The hard, hard lesson I've struggled to learn in sobriety goes like this: I know in my heart there's an abundance of love in this world for me, and that I'll always be okay. That's the basis of my spirituality. But every once in a while I decide that the love my higher power offers me isn't the kind of love I want. My higher power offers me friendship and companionship in abundance! And much of the time I accept that. But every once in a while, I'll separate myself from that and refuse to tap into it, when it's sitting right there! I back away from friendship and companionship, I refuse to engage with people who love me, and I start looking for romance. Which is such a pale imitation of real love. It's like candy, which is an imitation of real food, right?

So in looking for romance, I cut myself off from real love. I lose faith that what my higher power offers me is gonna be enough, and I tell myself I'm gonna be lonely.

But there's no reason to be lonely except that I don't pick up the phone, right? When I stop looking for romance and open myself to whatever love god is offering that day, I'm happy.

I used to go to the high school dance thinking I had to be stoned, because back then I couldn't take the risk of letting anyone know who I really was. But now I have an abundance of people who know who I really am. And sometimes I *still* separate myself from them! I *still* decide what I have isn't good enough. And I struggle to choose between the good food that's available and the candy I trick myself into thinking I need.

The good news is that I'm still progressing. I no longer date guys whose lives are in transition, and I spend a lot less time looking for sex or romance. I can enjoy the abundance of love I've been provided.

Sexual Surrender

Orgasm is so fun and freaky because it's an uncontrollable force of nature. It's like an electrical storm, a microburst inside our bodies. In the Middle Ages, the French called orgasm *le petit mort*—the little death—and like death, it can be a power greater than ourselves. Depending, of course, on how we think about it, and on how we treat it in our lives. If we try to control it, use it to escape, or routinely fake it, it bears looking at how we might work with the power instead of against it.

There's a lot of cultural meaning buried in the word "orgasm." Many people think it's a combination of the words "organ" and "spasm," but there's nothing in the history of the word that refers to spasms. The word "orgasm" does come from "organ," an ancient Greek word that originally meant "to swell as with moisture, be excited or eager." Force of nature—a power greater than any one of us.

The Chinese write their words in pictures, and the Chinese character for orgasm has three parts. The second and third parts translate to "high tide." The first part is a character itself made up of two words: the character for birth, and a picture of the human heart. So the Chinese word for orgasm gives the sense of a tide of energy that's part of human nature from our very beginnings.

The phrase "high tide" implies an ongoing cycle—if there's a high tide, then there's also a low tide. The tides are also a kind of ungovernable natural phenomenon. If it's as strong as a riptide, it could feel like it might kill us. And humans can reroute rivers, but we haven't yet successfully turned the tides, although we've spent considerable time and money building walls to control them, only to have them blown down.

Instead of trying to control that natural power and beauty—buying magazines that advertise promises like "How to Have Your Best Orgasm!!" or "Sex Shrink Tells You How To Make a Woman Orgasm" (clue: you can't), we might have a better time if we stopped struggling against the tide and started swimming with it. Which is to say, getting to know our own bodies and responses super well, and then finding language so we can tell our partners when and how to help us.

Orgasm: Variations on a Theme

"He can play me like a guitar," she told me. She is forty-three, divorced, with four years in recovery, and her boyfriend—the second she's had since she got out of an all-women's halfway house—is forty-two and has eight years. "It's crazy. I've never had anybody who can bring me to orgasm with their hands, and he can do that without fail. I don't know how he knows how to do it. It's like magic!"

He's not "doing it." The connection between them is. She trusts him. What's more, she really likes him. Which means she can surrender. So they're "doing it" together.

I tell her the kind of orgasm she's describing does not feel the same to me as a G-spot orgasm, which feels like a tsunami starting at the bottom of the ocean. The kind she had feels to me like a catamaran speeding across the surface of the water.

"Exactly!" she said.

She said she was very happy to talk to someone openly about her various kinds of orgasms and the different ways she's experienced them now that she has four years in recovery. Which means she has four years of actually being able to feel what's happening in her body—the high tides and low tides. When she was drinking and using, she couldn't feel those shifts in sexual energy.

She doesn't always stop with just one orgasm. She knows her body is capable of many orgasms, and recovery has allowed her to discern how high the tide is and how far she wants to swim. Sometimes she only wants one. Sometimes she wants more.

"By the third or fourth orgasm," she says, "the whole screaming-involuntarily-thing comes out."

The intensity of the language she uses to describe her experience stays with me after she leaves. *By the third or fourth orgasm. The whole screaming-involuntarily-thing.*

I say this not because I'm amazed that she can have many orgasms. Some people like many, and some don't care about having any, and most of us, including me, live in between those two extremes. Her words stay with me because they show her hard-earned understanding of herself. She has taken the principles of rigorous honesty, asking for help and speaking out loud, and brought them to bear on her sexuality. She has looked for language for her experiences. This is a woman who owns and lives inside her body, who swims in the tides even though they might sometimes scare her.

Surrender to powers greater than ourselves: that's a central principle of recovery, and she has learned to surrender.

Orgasm and the Brain

She has also described how much she enjoys just cuddling with this guy. She likes snuggling against him even more than she likes having orgasms with him. Which is surprising, she said, because when she was drinking and using she wasn't a cuddly person.

For people with histories of drug abuse, orgasms can be titillating and scary—they can be associated with kink, porn, and sex-for-pay. Both orgasm and drug abuse can cause some of the same things to happen in our bodies: our limbic brains release floods of dopamine in anticipation of pleasure, and the part of our brain that makes decisions shuts down. However, one important difference between drug abuse and orgasm, especially with someone we care about, is the surge of a neurochemical called oxytocin—the bonding hormone. It's also released in women during childbirth and breastfeeding, and in all of us when we see photos or read emails from people we love. (In fact, even looking at your dog in the eyes can release oxytocin in your brain!) Oxytocin has a calming, stabilizing effect on our bodies, and it strengthens human connection and trust. It's the cuddle chemical.

There's been lots of talk lately about how the millennial generation has discovered that casual sex and "chill" hookups as a way of life are not all that fulfilling. "[Chill] is a garbage virtue that will destroy the species," one millennial wrote.[22] I agree with this young one that we ought not to be denied our right to use Tinder in whatever way we please, and I support their refusal to call for a return to boomer-style monogamy. But I also think it's worth noting that, if younger generations are getting wise to the idea that a steady french-fry diet of Tinder hookups is a sorry-ass way to feed one's body and soul, it may be because that way of life goes against the higher power I've been calling "chemistry." Our bodies produce oxytocin when we have sex because it's to our serious evolutionary advantage to stick together as a species. Building a sex life of one-night stands—using sex as a drug, using sex to escape, using people— runs counter to that powerful inbuilt tide that can heal us if we surrender to it.

We Don't Have to Skinny-Dip (But We Can If We Want to)

I talked about orgasm with Greg Siegle, a professor of psychiatry who runs his own cognitive affective neuroscience lab at the University of Pittsburgh. Greg studies the way orgasm mediates emotional states such as depression. I said I'd learned while in active addiction how to use a vibrator to give myself multiple orgasms. He regarded me skeptically and said it's rare for people have more than one orgasm at a time, and that what might feel like multiple orgasms is basically surfing a tide of dopamine. What people call "multiple orgasm" is "really very carefully learning to manage the curve of your pleasure," he said. "My impression is that people who are multi-orgasmic such that they can have four in twenty minutes are learning to ride the dopamine wave."

"So how do they learn to do that?" I ask.

"A vibrator, many of them. By getting in touch with their bodies."

A question came up in several of my interviews: "Can I get addicted to my vibrator?" Greg said nobody knows, because the question hasn't been studied, but he uses vibrators in his own research, and he hasn't found anything that would indicate using a vibrator is dangerous. However, he said touching skin-to-skin makes us more sensitive connoisseurs of pleasure. "For example, if you take somebody who's taken some courses in wine tasting—they can't drink bad wine anymore," he said, oblivious of his analogy's irony. When we practice touching each other skin-to-skin, he said, we encourage "an appreciation for the subtlety that can be touch. And vibes don't match up in that way, generally."

Then something seemed to strike him. "People don't have to get naked to train in this kind of sensitivity, you know," he said. He stood up and asked whether it would be okay if he touched my neck. With a fingernail, he traced a slow line up the nape of my neck into my hairline. Then he did it again. As his fingernail moved, little tingles spread like ripples in a pond down my back and up into my scalp. It wasn't a "high tide," but it was a mini-flow of waves that relaxed my upper body.

Then he asked whether he could touch my fingers. I held out my left hand, and with the nails of his thumb and forefinger, he traced light lines from my wrist up either side of my ring finger. My body suddenly went limp with relaxation.

I asked where he'd learned to do that, and he said he'd been reading "some really old Chinese books."

He put my hand down. "Look," he said. "You're no longer as hyper-vigilant as you were. You can probably handle craving with more acumen than before. Your blood pressure has probably decreased. You not only relax, but you increase your ability to regulate your emotions and be able to handle things you otherwise couldn't."

You feel safe.

Relapse prevention in a nutshell.

"It's like *cafuné*," I mused, and I told him about *cafuné*.

"It's the same stuff," he agreed.

To practice this kind of sensitivity, we need other people. We need human connection. Trying to train ourselves to be sensitive to the life force and tidal energy that is orgasm is like trying to tickle yourself. As anthropologist Nina Jablonski says, we get the most benefit from grooming if others do it for us—and if we do it for others. So that makes it even more important to look for safe opportunities for mutual touch.

As members of *Homo sapiens*, we're uniquely qualified to touch each other's skin, and yet we live so much of our lives separated from each other in cubicles, cars, and corners of coffee shops. Let this be an unequivocal call for us to help each other heal from addiction by learning how to touch each other safely. How can we bring more human touch into our lives?

Equality in Sexual Surrender

This chapter pays more attention to women's orgasm than men's for a good reason: I've never heard of a statistic that claims any significant percentage of men have *never* experienced an orgasm. There are, however, numbers scattered hither and yon that purport to show that a significant fraction of women have spent their lives unable to enjoy this major reward of human sexuality.[23] I could quote a string of these figures here, but you know what? It would serve only to confuse the issue. Because as long as we insist on living outside of our bodies, how is a bunch of numbers really going to help us if we can't even talk with ourselves and each other about such extreme physical pleasure?

Telling our stories out loud with people we trust is the action that's going to break the silence and save us. The statistics might help us put our stories in context, but the numbers aren't what hold the stories' power.

True story: I talked with women who "faked it" and men who'd been faked out. Habitually faking it lets us save appearances at the cost of our integrity. So we drink and use to numb our self-hatred and lack of sexual satisfaction. And we wind up numbing the pleasure too.

True story: I've talked with recovering people who've had sex with upwards of thirty partners, and some with many more, who have had orgasms with less than five of those, and some with only two or three. They could not let themselves surrender to that tide with a person they did not know or like. "I've learned in recovery that it has to be someone I really trust," one told me. They fake it because it's easier than saying out loud that they don't trust their partners, because that's a very hard conversation for which to find language. And when we fake it as a way of life, we're on the road toward using.

It could be different.

We climb the stairs and start taking our clothes off. The more clothes we remove, the more naked our body feels, and the more the mind starts to control the fear of this nakedness.

Will she think I'm too short?

Will he think I'm too fat?

Will she like my penis?

I don't know what turns her on.

What if I come too fast?

What if I can't come at all?

I wish I had a drink or a drug.

We all have these thoughts, but we rarely say them out loud. The thoughts work against the tide.

The mind knows the layers of meaning—it's not just a simple matter of body-minus-clothing; it's the fact that getting naked means we're dropping the armor. We're literally stripping ourselves down. We're surrendering. Which is never easy for those of us with addiction.

The more naked we get, the more nervous we become—just another way of saying the more we allow our minds to take control of the situation. The more we fall back on self-will. The more we might want a drink, pill, joint, or line to take the edge off.

The edge is intimacy. It's the unknown. It's our involuntary physical response when someone we really like and trust touches our body, nuzzles our neck, winds fingers through our hair, strokes our skin, gives us *cafuné*.

What's happening in that bedroom in the dark, in each other's hearts, will never be known if one of us does not step out onto the razor's edge and risk some true words:

I'm not feeling this tonight.

I'm feeling this super-deep tonight! What about you?

No? Then what would you like?

What I really want is for us to just hold each other.

Can I ask for something different?

I want some lube.

Can we play with a toy too?

I would like it if you could touch me a little more lightly.

I would like it if you looked into my eyes sometimes.

How does what I'm doing with my hands make you feel?

I love it when you do that.

This is just me riffing here. There are as many other ways to have this conversation as there are people to imagine it. I want us all to imagine our own. That requires surrender.

Instead, many of us choose—out of the understandable fear of being sliced by the razor's edge—to resist. We choose to fumble around dumbly, fall asleep half-satisfied, lie awake not satisfied at all, and wonder what's wrong with us or with our partner.

And then we look outside of the relationship. Or we use. Or both.

"People who cheat, they're pursuing eroticism without realizing it," says Rosalyn Dischiavo, the sex educator. "They're looking for the aliveness piece, and cheating is one of the easiest ways to get there. We exile the erotic into the sexual, when in fact it's the other way around—the sexual is a subset of the erotic. The erotic is not sexuality, or even sensuality. It's pleasure, it's play. It's *aliveness.*

"Freud called eros *libido*. The East Indians call it *prana,* the Chinese call it *chi.* In our culture, it's been totally de-eroticized. Chi and prana are something in our culture that only yoga teachers do, in their breathy yoga-teacher voice: 'OK, everyone, *breeeeathe!*' It's a little ridiculous, because what we're really trying to do when we do it like that is get out of our bodies. But I'm interested in living inside my body erotically, because it enhances every part of my life. Orgasm is about eroticism and eroticism is about aliveness."

And aliveness is about recovery.

How to Surrender the Right Way

She told him, "Oh my god, you drive me out of my mind."

He said, smiling against her neck, "And into your body."

And then, she said, he moved his hands on her skin until she came.

When I heard this story, it occurred to me that, in the many years since I started my sexual exploration at seventeen, I have spent a good deal of time wondering whether I was having the "right" kind of orgasm, or whether I was having an orgasm at all. When I could escape the voices in my mind of my mother and various supposedly celibate priests insinuating what a slut I was for even thinking about sex, never mind trying to have it, I have always had rip-roaring orgasms—from my first romp with my first boyfriend, on through even abusive relationships in my twenties. I came so effortlessly that several guys I was with asked me, "You can have orgasms that easily?"

Which, of course, made me feel more like a slut. A good girl wouldn't be able to have such "easy" orgasms. I was "easy."

No: I wasn't easy. I could just surrender to that tide. I have to rename this experience—find other language for it—to let go of the story I've told myself for so long, a story that contributed to my drinking and drug use. I've spent more than three decades with this Whore Story on replay in my mind.

Last summer I asked sex educator Emily Nagoski about this critical voice in my mind. Nagoski talks about that "spectator" in your brain— the one who writes stories about your being a slut, your not being virile enough, your penis/breasts/whatever not being big enough, your belly/thighs/whatever not being small enough. One of Nagoski's top talking points is that women's bodies don't always reflect what's going on in their minds: in other words, our bodies aren't always as wet as we feel in our hearts.

I told her, I'm pretty proud of the fact that I've never faked orgasm. At least, I don't think I have. Or have I?

If I don't have a super-deep G-spot orgasm, am I faking it? Am I really surrendering?

"And is this 'spectating'?" I asked Nagoski. "If I decide 'in my brain' that I've had an orgasm, does that mean I've had one? Or am I faking it?"

"If you liked it, and you wanted it, you did it right," she said. "Yes. Yes."

How to surrender the right way? We find out what we like. Then we ask for it. Yes.

. . .

Queries for Discussion

Sexual Surrender

☐ How has my ability to be inside my body while having sex changed since I got into recovery? How have my sexual preferences changed? How have they remained the same?

☐ Does having sexual pleasure scare me? Why? Does it scare me because it reminds me of my drug use?

☐ How is my experience of sexual pleasure different from using drugs?

☐ How can I bring my spiritual practice to bear on my sexuality? How can my spiritual practices guide me in surrendering and accepting my capacity for pleasure and connection?

☐ When have I faked pleasure in bed? Why do I want to deceive my partners? Do I hold an attitude about my own sexuality that leads me to fake orgasm? Under what conditions could I be honest with my partner about what pleases me?

☐ What have I been secretly longing to say to my partner in bed?

MARIA LUZ

What We Stole from Others and Ourselves

Forty-four / Seven years in recovery

My mom always knew I wasn't your typical little boy. And I always knew I was different. But I would never, ever have thought I'd wind up making money as a sex worker.

I got into that lifestyle because my stepfather and I weren't getting along, and I ran away from home at about nineteen. I just picked up and went to Santa Monica Boulevard. In the nineties, that's where all the gay boys and all the trans women traded sex for money. It was lively back then. It's not the same now—there's a lot of cops around. Back then, you were free to work the boulevard, and you could make a living.

I met a drag queen named Venus Gloss who took me in. She introduced me to the life. She said, "You just go in a car and make your money." But the thing is, to do that, I always had to be drunk. I was in my early twenties.

I got arrested in '94, when I was twenty-three, and that's when I started doing crystal meth. While I was working the boulevard, I was also trying to go to school. I lived near Fountain and Highland in Hollywood, and at four-thirty in the morning I had to catch the bus. One of my roommates said, "Why don't you try some of this stuff? It'll wake you up."

My meth use got so bad so fast that one of my professors took me aside and told me my grades were dropping and asked me what the hell was going on. I was expelled until the next semester.

Which just meant I had more time to use, right?

And in order to use, I had to work the boulevard. To work the boulevard, I had to get in cars. To get in cars, I had to be drunk.

For years, I just circled around and around in that spiral.

I never got arrested for tricking. I got arrested for stealing.

When I did crystal meth, I used to steal. It didn't even have to be stuff I wanted—it was mostly just stupid shit. Then one of my sidekicks had this brilliant idea: we'd go steal stuff at one Nordstrom's and then go to another one and return it. We actually did that. We went to San Francisco. We went into Nordstrom's, but we were so obviously fucked up that they were watching us through the cameras. The undercover people arrested me and put me in a holding tank in San Francisco. I got out on my own recognizance and took a Greyhound bus back to Hollywood.

My last arrest was that same year. I stole a trick's credit card and used it to try to buy a bunch of groceries. It was two or three in the morning, and I went to the supermarket at Third and Vermont and filled up two carts full of stuff. Mind you, I was homeless!—I *looked* homeless, and I had no place to put all that stuff.

When I got to the counter, I presented them with this trick's credit card. As soon as I handed it over, I knew something bad was gonna happen. When I tried to leave the store, two cops were waiting for me. They took me to the Glass House—the Parker Center PD in downtown LA. Then they hauled me out to county jail. At that time, if you were trans, they took you to the county jail near Magic Mountain—that's where they used to house transsexuals. They said taking me out of the city was for my own good. I was in there for maybe three months in a cell with another trans woman.

That experience made me understand why they do the things they do to trans women in jail. Like being told to bend over, crack a smile and cough—being a trans woman and being ordered to do that in front of men was one of the most humiliating times of my life. Along with being put in a cage while other inmates were being brought in.

They don't *want* you to go back. And I've never gone back since then.

I was clean when I got out, but I didn't stay clean.

I met up with my mom—she's my rock and my anchor; she's been there for me from day one. She came to pick me up when I was released. She got me a place—a hotel room at first, then she rented me a house in Hollywood. I got a job. I wasn't selling my body, but for a while I worked as a phone-sex operator.

And right after my mom got me that house, I started going out with a guy named Bruce. I could see that he was doing drugs, but because I hated myself, I moved him into my house. I was not in my right mind. We'd been together two or three months, and one day I was cleaning the house and putting clothes into the dresser, and I saw a book about HIV. So I asked him about it, and that's when he told me he was HIV positive.

So I got tested, and guess what.

And *still* I didn't dump him. I stayed with him for another three years. That just goes to show where my self-esteem was at the time. The messed-up part was, eventually *he* dumped *me!* Once again, I was dumped for a genetic woman.

So I stopped doing meth, but I continued to drink.

I've known my sponsor since before I got clean and sober. He likes both trans and genetic women, and when we first met he liked me, but I made it clear that I didn't like him that way. But we stayed friends. All those years I was drinking, he always told me, "If you continue drinking the way you do, you'll end up doing crystal meth again."

So in 2009, I got so drunk that I was bar-hopping. And you know how, when you're drunk, you'll say yes to anything? Well, this guy at some bar offered me some meth. I hadn't done meth in a long time, and I'd never smoked it. But that night we were drunk and we began smoking the shit out of the meth. We smoked for a couple days.

I can't even tell you how many men I was with in the four days I was awake. I had random men just coming in and out of my house. I was so high for so long that I thought there were bugs crawling in my hair, and I cut it all off. When I woke up out of that run, I was in a psych ward and basically bald.

And that run seven years ago was the last time I took a drink or a drug.

My life has changed since then.

After I cleaned up and started working seriously with my sponsor to face the facts of my history, it became very clear that, for me, doing drugs and alcohol has to do with my father leaving my mother for her best friend—my babysitter—when I was very young.

My addiction also has to do with being molested by my stepfather. It began when I was maybe six or seven. He had me suck him off when my mom wasn't home.

Seven years old. That's thirty-seven years ago.

The memory is quite vivid, even to this day.

I've been single for three years.

I sometimes try to meet guys. It's difficult to find a man who's willing to take me out. I don't know whether it's their way of saying they're uncomfortable with dating T-girls, but when they do send pictures, they always hide their faces. Even after I tell them, "Please do not text me X-rated pictures of your penis," the first thing they do is text me pictures of their penis. Maybe they just want to have sex. Maybe they think I just want to have sex.

And of course they always want to know what's between my legs. What I hate the most is when people ask, "Are you pre-op or post-op?" But I'm not just an object. I do have feelings. I want to have relationships, just like anyone else. Before I got clean and sober, those kinds of questions wouldn't have bothered me as much as they do now. I probably would have just answered them, because I didn't love and value myself.

Today, I have a clean mind. What I always say now is, "My genitalia have nothing to do with my gender identity." That's important. The only person who needs to know what's between my legs is the person I'm having sex with.

I've gone to Alcoholics Anonymous and Crystal Meth Anonymous. Working the Steps helped me so much. What's helped most is working them with my sponsor, especially Steps Four through Nine. I've learned to see my part in things that hurt me and in things that I did wrong, and to make amends to people for hurting them.

I remember doing that Eighth Step and writing my amends list. My sponsor said, "This is fine and this is great, but there's one person you're missing here."

I thought, "I can't remember—who else might I be missing?"

He said, "Maria Luz, you're missing making amends to yourself."

The moment my life really changed was when I forgave my stepfather for molesting me. The change came from the fact that I was able to let things go.

I'm very grateful to my sponsor. He's the one who planted the seed of recovery in my life. When I did all that meth and was taken to the hospital in 2009, and I finally admitted I had a problem, he was the first person I called. I told him the truth about being molested and how I'd worked the boulevard. I took the Fourth and Fifth Steps with him on all that stuff.

No matter what, I tell him everything.

I told him about my boyfriend Andy. We were together for a year and a half, and he was the last guy I was seeing before I got clean. He cheated on me. Later, when I told my sponsor about my resentments about that relationship, I realized my own part in its destruction: during the last year before we broke up, I was no longer intimate with him. I just pulled away. It wasn't that I wasn't in love with him, but I made school and work a priority and didn't make time for him. So then I could see why he cheated.

What I found out was this: I worked the boulevard for two years, and the fact that I tricked continues to hurt me today. I mean, my body is supposed to be a temple, right? A temple is a place where you keep valuable things, sacred things. And back then, I had no problem just flinging open the doors of that temple for those men and selling them what was inside. Which means I really stole from my own temple.

On second thought, it's not really accurate to say that I had no problem doing it. I knew it was hurting me, because I had to be drunk to get it done.

Doing that business desensitized me in some ways to emotions—to my feelings and the feelings of other people. One of my boyfriends once pointed out, "You treat this relationship like you're working." He was right—that whole business really fucked with my ability to be intimate with other human beings, even with people I love and who love me.

The thing with Andy took a toll on how I feel about honesty, manipulation, and lying. I'm just much more cautious about starting all over again.

I've dated since then, but I haven't had a long-term boyfriend since 2012. There was Mike from 2009 to 2012, and then Ryan in 2013, but only for about six months. So I've had two relationships in the seven years I've been clean and sober—one long-term and one short-term.

Ryan lived in San Diego, two and a half hours away. He would pay for me to go to San Diego every other weekend, but that got kind of old. That was the only reason why we broke up.

Since then, I've dated here and there. But most men see us T-girls as objects. That's the sad reality of our lives as trans women.

Today I have three sponsees. Taking people through the Steps takes me away from my own self-involved thinking. Because sometimes I get really depressed. I'll meet a guy, I'll talk to him for a week, and then I make a date with him and he doesn't fucking show up! But I always have to remember their attitude shows more about them than it does about me.

In fact, their attitude shows nothing about me.

Whenever I'm depressed, I try to shift the focus in my attitude away from myself. There are times I don't want to go to a meeting, but instead of giving in to that attitude I take contrary action. I call my sponsees; I see how they're doing. I find people who are having a more difficult time than I am. I know I'll find someone else. I don't just want a boy-toy boyfriend.

A boy-toy boyfriend is one where you take care of the guy financially, and he doesn't work. I know trans women who are like that—they settle for boy toys. I always tell them, "You're worth a lot more than that." I honestly don't get why they'd want that. I think it shows they have low self-esteem. Trans women, straight women—there's no reason why you need to support a man.

And there are other times when I go on a date and there's just no chemistry. I go on a first date and they don't look like their pictures. Sometimes my friends are like, "You're too shallow." I say, "I'm not shallow, I just know what I like." Just because I'm trans, does that mean I should have to do without physical chemistry? I'm still a woman!

The bottom line for me is, I want somebody who will love me for who I am as a person.

That means I want a guy who's going to respect me in public. I've gone out with guys who aren't comfortable in their own skins, who aren't going to be comfortable being with a trans woman. If they don't want to take me out in the daytime, that's a clue: it's usually because they think it will be more obvious that I'm trans.

If a guy isn't comfortable enough with himself to take me out in the daytime, I no longer think it means I'm not pretty or can't pass for a girl. I *know* I'm pretty, and the way I live now, I feel good about living inside my body. I think it means he doesn't care for *himself* enough to feel secure taking me out. I *look like* a girl, I *am* a girl, and I'm secure in that knowledge. And I want to be with a man who's secure inside himself.

Sometimes I have to tell people I'm trans. I'm a passable girl—people usually think I'm a girl. Unless you're gay or you know about my lifestyle, people don't usually know I'm a trans woman. If I'm walking down the street and a guy wants my number, I don't tell him right there—I tell him over the phone. I mean, it's hot when a guy wants my number in the middle of the street!—but it can also be dangerous, and since I got clean and sober, I'm no longer willing to endanger myself. I'm no longer a young girl—in your twenties you're fearless, but I'm forty-four, and I'm sober, and I value my life today.

I have sex, but honestly I'm not a very sexual person. I don't have sex even weekly. When I'm in a relationship, I'm okay with having sex twice or three times a month. I don't know if it's my hormones or what, but I'm okay with my level of desire.

But my sponsor told me he thinks I need to seek outside help. What he's noticed in my relationships is this: I may be really into a guy, but once I know he's with me, it's like I detach sexually. My sponsor thinks that has a lot to do with my childhood. I detach when the relationship is getting serious, because I'm afraid of being abandoned. Or hurt in some way, stolen from.

When I speak to groups, I always tell people that you might think we don't have much in common, but we do have something in common. When we take our first drink or drug, we don't know what's going to happen. We've all done things to hurt people. And we've all taken what's not ours to take, even when what we've stolen was stolen from ourselves.

Amends

. . . .

Here is a truth that needs to be universally acknowledged: we hurt others, and others hurt us.

For more than a year, I've been participating in live worldwide video chats about sex in recovery.[24] I've been putting out feelers online about sexual politics and the ways they affect recovery. As I listen to people online and in real-life interviews, many of the stories I've heard about sexual harms and amends address two basic themes:

- *I'm in a marriage or committed relationship and I cheated on my partner.* I did it by talking about sex with someone online, or by sexting people on my phone, or by hooking up with people in real life. I ended my relationship because my partner deserves someone better than me—or I'm still in my relationship, but there's no real connection because I can't be honest. In any case, I can't forgive myself. If you're still listening, I know you have judgments of me because of what I've done, and I think you should judge me, because I'm a terrible person.

- *I fear intimacy.* I haven't had sex in years. I avoid all sexual connection. I worry that if I get into a relationship I'll screw it up and get hurt again. Something inside me says I'd be better off not having sex, but another part wants deep connection and communication with another person. That second part wants to be touched and held. It wants to look into someone else's eyes. It says, "I want the whole thing. I don't want to be just two bodies slamming up against each other—I want to actually make love."

177

> And okay, I know I sound like a moron when I talk about "making love," but that's the way I feel.

In other words: we hurt others, and others hurt us.

When we hurt others, and when we no longer use drugs or behaviors to numb our emotions, we might feel the kind of remorse and self-recrimination expressed in the first theme above. We feel afraid of continuing to hurt others, and we resent ourselves because of our past actions.

When others hurt us, and we no longer numb our emotions, we might feel like walling ourselves off from the rest of humanity. We think, "Maybe I'm just incapable of being in a relationship." We may not even believe that, but we feed that thought anyway, because we think it keeps us safer than looking for what we want, which is to find connection with another human being as expressed in the second theme. We're so afraid of not finding that connection—and paradoxically, maybe we're also simultaneously afraid of finding it—that we decide it's better just to stay away from everyone.

Both these attitudes are grounded in self-loathing, and in denial of a truth of human experience, which is that we hurt each other. And some of those hurts—some of the biggest, most painful hurts—are sexual. Part of recovery is learning how to negotiate that fact without turning around and hurting ourselves, so that we can live with peace of mind.

The best way to make amends isn't just to apologize, but to change the hurtful behavior. But if you Google "making sexual amends," you come up with half a million results, the vast majority on the topic of sex addiction. But we're not talking here about sex addiction—we're talking about making sexual amends inside recovery from addiction to substances.

So how do we do that? There are as many ways as there are individuals. In this book we've already heard some people tell how recovery has led them to change their behavior with regard to sex. Samuel, for example, no longer uses porn or participates in the economy of sex-for-pay. Dré no longer uses women strictly for his own sexual satisfaction, or for street cred among his friends. He, Joseph, and Maria Luz are HIV positive and they all make amends to themselves by taking the medications that keep them healthy and by discussing their health with potential partners.

Being honest with partners about HIV could feel degrading, but carried out with an attitude of honesty, it becomes an act of humility—of deep knowledge and acceptance of oneself. This builds self-respect.

So the process of amends has the power to lead us away from self-denigration, self-hatred, and other caustic attitudes that might make us want to numb our feelings. When we live in an attitude of humility and self-respect, we're less likely to want to use. We strengthen our ability to help others.

The subject of amends is raised throughout this book as people talk about the sexual harms they've inflicted on others and themselves. I hope these stories will open the way for you to imagine how you might find peace with the deeply human experience of having harmed others. For the people I spoke with, that process usually began with talking honestly with at least one other person about the damage they thought they'd done and imagining ways of changing their behavior for the better.

To begin with, many of the people I talked with were directed to write lists of people they'd treated in sexually selfish ways. Sometimes the lists themselves, if they were extensive, presented opportunities that were hard to resist. "When I did my sex inventory, I seriously wanted to text everybody on that list," one young man told me. "My sponsor was like, 'What are you trying to get out of contacting all these people? You can't do that. That's not what this list is for.' I'd tricked myself into thinking I'd just say hi and see how they were. It was for nothing good! I wanted them all to see how awesome I look now. I was just going to pick them all up."

Infidelity

Since delusion, distortion of the truth, and outright lying are part and parcel of addiction, one of the ways we hurt others is by breaking our commitments to them and then lying about it or hiding it. I spoke with several people who had experienced infidelity on one side or the other. Hearing about, or admitting, infidelity can fracture trust between two people and damage self-esteem individually, even if amends are made and the couple manages to stay together. Magdalene talks about this in the chapter on honesty.

In the chapter on trauma, Diana, sixty-two, talks about her child-hood sexual abuse. She later had lots of compulsive sex to control her feelings about being abused. "I was engaged two times before I met my husband, Paul," she said. "I had multiple affairs while I was engaged to those other men. I'd just go out and bring somebody home pretty much every weekend. But I wanted to find some normality, and Paul seemed like the right guy for the job. So my intentions in marrying Paul were probably pretty crappy to begin with."

She learned about her intentions by practicing recovery principles and talking with people she trusts, including her therapist, friends, and sponsors.

Like many people I talked with who committed infidelity—who, as one person put it, were "infidels"—Diana's compulsion to cheat didn't disappear after she got married. "Sexually, my husband has always been terrific," she said. "But in looking back after I got sober, there were twenty years during our marriage when I never had sex with Paul when I wasn't drunk or using something. That's how our relationship started out, right out of the gate. We used and drank together. We did drugs together, too, but he was a slacker compared to me. It became kind of a joke—'Oh boy, Diana's drunk tonight, we can have sex.' We had a lot of sex when we first met, and then our sex life started to hit the rocks. So I looked for it elsewhere. I had two affairs outside of my marriage. It started probably ten years in. Paul was traveling a lot, and one night I went to a bar, and I knew the bartender there, and I just got fucked up and went back to his place. And then a friend of ours came to visit, and he stayed at the house, and I pretty much targeted him too.

"When I started cheating like that, I really went off the rails with my addiction. I constantly drank to blackout. I'd leave the house in the middle of the night and go looking for drugs. I had a dealer in a nearby neighborhood. I'd spend a lot of time between my house and there. When I couldn't get anything there, I'd go pretty often to an alley in a rough part of town where I knew someone would get me coke, Quaaludes, crank, Vicodin to fuck me up. And I drank constantly. On top of what I bought on the street, I drank a fifth of vodka a day.

"I would do sexually inappropriate things all the time, and always when I was drunk. Like, I threw myself onto my sister's boyfriend. It got to the point that Paul didn't even want to have sex with me when I was drunk."

I asked Diana whether she's ever told her husband about these other men.

"He never knew I was with other people. I never told him. He still doesn't know. There's that phrase, 'Made direct amends except when to do so would injure them or others'? If I told him, it would crush him. Especially since he knew some of these guys."

She said that once she got into recovery, her husband supported her by going to therapy with her and driving her to meetings. Many people are not fortunate enough to find partners who are willing to support their recovery. Should she have admitted her infidelity to her partner? That's a decision she made for herself, and that each of us has to make for ourselves. In making amends, we may consider that humility asks us not to make ourselves the star of a destructive drama: "I'm an addict, and here is the damage I did to you!!" It's also important to keep in mind that we can't turn back the clock and make life as it was before addiction—that's a fantasy. We live in real time.

"Living" Sexual Amends

I ask Adrian, twenty-eight, with seven years in recovery, to talk about the kinds of amends she's made in recovery. Adrian has an asymmetrical gamine pink haircut, a diamond in her nostril, a beaten sterling cuff on her wrist, and her toenails are painted with tiny soccer balls. She goes to Alcoholics Anonymous, and she can't resist pointing a finger at the Big Book's 578 words on sex. "I love that it's on page sixty-nine," she says. "For real? I see you guys! You creepy motherfuckers! Look, I've read Bill W.'s biography. I see him, tripping on acid, sleeping with all kinds of chicks. My man, Bill," she says fondly.

Adrian is now engaged to her girlfriend. As a young woman who has had many sexual partners, and who has a great capacity to enjoy sex, she's taken her time to settle down. So if amends are changed behavior, amends for Adrian in this context involve feeling all her feelings—such as fear of boredom, and also her desire to explore commitment—without either cheating or hiding. "Part of my thing with sex is trying to figure out how to have the crazy, exciting rush with the same person for a long time," she says. "She doesn't always turn me on. It's been tough. I don't have the answers to it. It's like the next great journey for me—sticking with someone. Having sex with one person, only, for a year and a half. That's the longest I've ever had sex with just one person. The longest before that was three months.

"I'm very principled. I don't like fantasizing about other people when we have sex. I don't like not being there physically or emotionally when we have sex. I feel like that would be dishonest of me. That's what I mean about honesty and spiritual principles with sex. Because I think sex is a beautiful, pure, god-given thing. I say 'god' because it's shorthand.

"I wanted to talk to you about sex because sex was a huge part of my sobriety story and my faith. And when I tell my lead I talk a lot about sex and spirituality. I *love* sex. And I'm saying, 'I'm gonna own this. I can have sex and no one's gonna take away sex, because sex is really fucking cool! It's not the *best* thing, but it's really cool.' And I'm excited about the conversations that are starting to happen about sex."

．　．　．

Queries for Discussion

Amends

☐ How do I understand "harm" in terms of sexuality?

☐ When have I used sexuality for destructive purposes, whether I was aware of that motivation or not?

☐ If I wasn't aware of that motivation, what blinded me to it? What steps can I take to make sure I don't do that damage again?

☐ What are the names of people I have hurt through sex or sexual behavior? For what reasons might I put myself on that list?

☐ If, because of blackouts or other causes, I can't remember the names of everyone I may have hurt or the harms I inflicted, what would it take for me to begin to welcome myself to the human race and forgive myself, so that I can move on, live with peace of mind, and enjoy the pleasure of human connection that sexuality offers?

Recovery: The Sexual Revelation

Many of the stories in this book so far have explored what happens sexually when the body wakes up and the mind clears. At some point in recovery, many people move past the stage of awakening and into agency—the ability to truly act on one's own behalf. In the three stories that close out this book, we meet a trio of recovering people who have grounded themselves in their bodies and their sexual identities. Even though they are at different stages in their lives and relationships, they're no longer just waking up. They've been using recovery principles long enough to inquire into themselves, and now they're beginning to realize and express their own potential. Including their sexual potential.

At that point, sex in recovery becomes about ownership, beginning with our bodies and our experiences. Self-possession.

It's about eating the fruit of the tree of knowledge: not waffling between binaries such as good and evil, but discerning levels of truth. It's accepting that state of mind called peace.

Sex in recovery is a revelation that comes from forces that are greater than we are, and that are also, paradoxically, part and parcel of us. One example is the mysterious healing power of humor. In the first of the next three stories, Tom recalls being arrested for having oral sex on a park bench. His long-term recovery lets him look at that memory with wry humor. His ability to see the pathos in the relationship that led to that incident doesn't preclude his ability to find it funny. Nor does he beat himself up for getting collared for a public blow job. He can hold feelings of amusement and wretchedness in one hand. The ability to carry conflicting feelings, and the capacity to avoid self-disgust about poor decisions, are marks of recovery, and of maturity.

Tom has also made it his way of life to be rigorously honest about the physical and psychological limitations of his disability. First, he has to be honest with himself, and that can be difficult for those of us who engaged in deceit for so long inside our active illness. The residual self-mistrust of his addiction is evident in his speech: He says, of a period of time when he was abused as a child, "My memory is. . ." As if it's his word against his abuser's. As if it's his word against that of the bully in his mind, the bully who tells him he can't trust his memory. For many years, Tom had hidden the truth of the abuse he experienced for so long that when he talks about it now, it still feels unfamiliar and, well, in some ways *wrong*. He spent many years drinking and using to keep the door shut on those stories. Recovery has shown him that he might sometimes *feel* wrong, but as long as he tells the truth to the best of his ability—and there is no Perfect Truth—he can know he's right with himself.

Recovery has allowed both Tom and Olivia to see sex as one of the last oases of truly creative, mutual playtime for those big kids known as adults. I mean okay, go plug in your Call of Duty or Minecraft, but accept that you'll be by yourself while you hit the joysticks. If someone touches your skin while you're fingering those little electronic knobs?—it will be a distraction, not a pleasure. There's nothing wrong with a little alone time, but recovery has allowed Tom and Olivia to discover the sheer fun of sexual connection with their partners. Their attitudes toward sex have run a few laps on the track past "good, giving, and game": they're rooted in the damn hard work of self-acceptance, a commitment to learn about their own desires and limitations and those of their partners, and above all a recognition that if they want intimacy they have to communicate, and communication is the first-born child of honesty.[25] Tom, for example, is one straight man who has bothered to learn about female anatomy and how to touch it, and he knows more about some parts than I do, which is saying a lot. Rather than being ashamed of the particular time in his life before he got sober, recovery has shown Tom that he can build on his overall sense of knowledge and understanding—and that extends to schooling himself on how to please his partner and putting that knowledge to very good use.

(He says his wife sometimes kids him that she's going to take out an insurance policy on his hands.)

As for Olivia, one thing being sober has taught her about her sexuality is that she enjoys varieties of sex that she'd never thought she could. In recovery, if we do the painstaking archeology of discerning and telling the truth, we find out who we really are, and eventually our old, false selves lose their power to incite fear or shame.

In this book's last story, Gabriel tells what he learned when he watched his downtown New York City home group lose men, one by one, as they died during the AIDS epidemic of the mid-1980s. This is not the story of Gabriel's own sexual experience, but of how the community he found in recovery formed—or re-formed—his character: he became a man who could act in his own best interests, including his sexual interests. The community he describes is radical in its ability to accept challenges, tolerate discord, forgive mistakes, and give love without strings attached. This home-group recovery community provided those who were dying, and those who lived, with the power to face the humiliation and pain of disease, the torment of social judgment and familial rejection, the agony of dying and the bewilderment of survival—all without using.

That's power. That power is a revelation, when it is found.

Let's meet these three people and hear about their own hard-won revelations.

. . .

TOM

The Self-Respect Earned in Recovery

Forty-eight / Eight years in recovery

Here's what my relationship was like with the woman I was seeing when I finally got sober.

Barbara and I were arrested for public indecency in a city park. She was giving me head on a picnic bench. I ended up in jail, but not for that. They hauled me in on the sex charge, but they locked me up on a past bench warrant for something I'd done a long time before. And I was five months sober when all that happened.

I'd started dating Barb several months after my car accident, and despite all the damage I'd done to my body in that crash, I didn't quit drinking and using for another year and a half. Barb was married, and I was with her for four years. For two of those, we were drinking buddies and had crazy-good sex. Despite the fact that she was married, I thought the awesome sex meant we loved each other and belonged together, but I can see now that it was really just safety—for me, at least. I've been looking for a mom forever. I hate and blame my mother because of what she did to me, but then I go out and look for someone to take care of me, and give me rules, and guide me, and love me when I make mistakes. And Barb did all of that.

Sexually, from the very beginning, we had an insane amount of fun. I mean—*best sex of my life.* We were willing to try anything sexually because we had the same disrespect for sex, and because we were looking for each other's approval. We felt like partners in crime. Which is curious, because I don't feel like "partners in crime" now with my wife. Sexually, I think my wife looks to me to be the leader. I sometimes say, "It would be really nice if you'd be the aggressor." And she'll try. I mean, when she gets totally turned on and flushed, she comes into that kind of role with a fervor. But generally, it's not her nature.

But with Barb, there was a complete sexual ease—every kink matched perfectly and I totally mistook that for love.

I only figured out about a year ago that it wasn't love at all. I mean, getting arrested for oral sex on a bench in a public park?—I still think that's just funny and stupid, but everything about my relationship with Barb in that period of getting sober is sad. We both wanted it to evolve with our hearts, but we couldn't change in our feelings past the resentments that were growing because I'd decided to get sober and she was still drinking. So I felt trapped. She felt trapped with this guy who—you know how, in early sobriety, you become even more needy and squirmy. She felt trapped with that.

And it took me seven years of recovery, seven years of hard introspective work, to understand that that kind of sex was not love.

I think I would have become an alcoholic no matter what. I'm Russian on one side and Irish on the other. My genes are loaded.

My father was an alcoholic, and I wanted to be just like my father. But both my parents were very ill equipped to raise kids. They were both abused when they were children, and they were both addicts. My mother in particular made a series of really bad choices. I remember my mother taking her time soaping my penis in the bathtub. Another time, as a child, I pulled my zipper up and got my foreskin caught, and she decided to kiss it and make it better. I can't think about those memories without thinking they were sexual.

Then there was the other side of her behavior. When I was five, my mother picked up a potted plant by the leaves and hurled it at me from across the room. She missed, but still: any kid would wonder, *What did I do to make her do that?*—I can't even remember. Some five-year-old behavior, like spilling chocolate milk. And then she came toward me and bent down close to my face, clenched her teeth, and said, *"I wish I'd never fucking had you."*

So I made two decisions when I was very young: One, that I would not love or respect my mother, and two, that no god was going to save me. And based upon those decisions, the only thing I knew to do to comfort myself—which is something I've seen my father and grandfather do—was to put something in my mouth. I ate my way through despair. So I'd get heavy: I'd make myself ugly, and I built a wall of fat around myself. A lot of people say only women do that, but it's absolutely not true.

And by the time I was twelve, I was drinking.

Freddie Flanagan lived in the house behind us. He was in his mid-twenties when I was a kid. He worked as the bagger at our neighborhood grocery store. He was heavyset—big and powerful.

There's a playground near my old school, and when I was six, I was allowed to ride my bike there by myself. A number of times, Freddie got off the city bus when he saw me there. He'd walk over and angrily tell me, "I wanna show you something." And he'd reach into his pants—this is in clear view of the school—and he'd pull his hand back up and say, "I have a gun." It was his hand. But he'd hold his pointed finger to my head and pretend to shoot me through the head.

Then he'd say, "I'm a doctor. You have to trust me. I have to check your heartbeat." And in front of the school and all the traffic on the main road, he'd put his hand down the front of my shirt and touch my chest. And then he'd put it down the back of my shirt and touch my back.

My memory is, a number of times he took me through the back door of his house into his basement, and he forced me to go down on him. And I never told *anyone.* Not until I was thirty-one years old, when I told my brother, whose wife is a drug and alcohol therapist, and he said, "We have to tell Mom and Dad."

So my brother and his wife took me out to see my parents. When I was finished telling my mother, she started crying, and she turned to me and said, "You think it's *my* fault. You blame *me!*" And my brother stood up and said, "You can't talk like this to Tom." His wife got up and walked out of the house. Later she came back and told my parents that I would need some therapy to help me deal with these memories. Everybody was like, "Okay."

And then we never talked about it again.

So it's probably no surprise that it's very hard for me to trust people in relationships. Only rarely in my life has any other person brought me to orgasm—it takes a lot for me to trust the other person enough and let them see me that way. So that lack of trust takes away from the other person's power. In my earlier relationships, I couldn't give the women the benefit of seeing me get off. And it's easier for a woman to fake it than it is for a guy, right? I wanted to be honest with my partners, but that meant they would realize how damaged I was. When they saw that I couldn't or wouldn't get off with them, they were like, "You're *broken,* man."

Because of what happened in that basement with Freddie, anytime I've ever been with a woman, it's taken a while for me to be comfortable in sexual situations. Like, I can't get erect right away because I'm so fearful of anyone touching me. It's not like I can walk into a date and if things are going great and we're in the car—it's not like she can just pull my pants down and I'll have a hard-on. I have to feel safe. I have to get Freddie out of my head, but somehow my body still remembers. My wife can't touch the backs of my legs, for example, because that's where *he* touched me.

To feel safe I have to let myself talk about it. When my wife and I first started dating, as I'm kissing her I whispered, "You know that I was abused." I said, "I need to go really slow, and I need to gain trust in you. It has nothing to do with you. But understand that for me to participate—for my penis to participate with us—I have to gain some confidence, and it's all about me feeling safe. I really want to fool around, I really want to be with you, and there's no reason why we can't play and have mutual satisfaction."

And she was like, "I'm fine with that. I like you—I'm not dating your sexuality, I'm dating *you*."

And the simplicity and honesty of her response kind of blew me away. It gave me a little bit of a swagger.

My old girlfriend Barbara had to push me out of her life, and it broke my heart. I'd never had a broken heart without being able to take a drink or a drug. I thought it was love, but really it was just devastating fear.

I moved back to the apartment that I'd maintained but not lived in for two years. I spent whole days in a fetal position on my bed. I wasn't showering. I wasn't taking care of myself. And my sponsor—he's a stay-at-home dad—he would come to my place with his one-and-a-half-year-old baby and tell me to get my ass out of bed, and he'd drag me down to the car and drive me to his house. And I would just lie on his couch and cry.

I started going to meetings every day—started hanging out with recovery friends again. But I was so crushed all I talked about was that she'd finally walked away from me.

I had a few relationships after that, before I met my wife. I had a lot of one-night stands. I had a platonic relationship with someone in recovery, and we'd go to movies and hang and talk. And then I had a not-so-platonic relationship with another woman who was a continual backslider, who was very attractive, and who, I understand, has had relationships with many men. While there was a little bit of playing around, there was never any major sex. To my knowledge, she's gone back to drinking and using.

With all the women I've ever been with, more than I wanted sex, I think I craved being touched. I want to be held, and I want to feel safe. Even four years in with my wife, I don't think I truly relax enough. Sometimes I think I'm not ever going to relax.

The kind of sexual ease Barb and I had—I long to have that in my marriage. My wife and I are starting to get that, but it's only after four years of being together and only when she and I are doing some kind of body-work.

A lot of it is just Western versions of Eastern stuff—hand-holding, breathing exercises. Some Tantric stuff, where I'll bring her to the brink and teach her about plateaus and raising the orgasm, raising it and raising it. I can do that with myself to some point, but my body is fighting me now. Because of the accident, and the nerve damage, I just can't attain that feeling because the nerve endings aren't there. Still, that level of trust and attention—it feels like what love and sex are supposed to be like.

And all these ways of playing sexually that I've never felt secure enough to let anyone else play into? Or I did them, but I felt so uncomfortable?—In our case, we'll just look at each other and ask, "Did that work for you?"

"Nah, not so much."

"Okay, well, let's try something else."

In the four years we've been together, our sex life has morphed and changed. About six months into dating, we started to have intercourse. Before quitting drinking and using, you think I would have waited *six months* before having sex? No way. And the self-respect I've earned in recovery has translated into this relationship. One example is, given my physical disability, the amount of nerve damage caused by the accident, I take five milligrams of an erectile dysfunction medication each day. And I also sometimes use a band around my penis. It helps me last longer. With Barbara, I was frightened to death of what she thought about me, and I couldn't do these things that help me sexually. This was a huge emotional shortcoming: I was afraid of judgments and disapproval about my body and my health. But with my wife, I've been like, "This is who I am, and this is what I have to do to be who I am. Let's work toward better health for me." I mean, if I can't be myself to get off in front of my wife, why am I married?

The work of recovery, the commitment to honesty, has helped me feel like my wife and I are in the same mind-space together. We're working on something mutual, and it's respectful, not just of each other, but of what sex is, what it means, what it's for.

OLIVIA

Owning Your Sexuality

Forty-four / Eleven years in recovery

I was raised in a very sex-positive home. There was sex education from an early age. It was extremely nonjudgmental. When I say "sex-positive," I mean that sex was represented to me as something that I would want, that I should want, and that I would probably enjoy. And that all that was okay. And that it was very important to avoid getting pregnant.

My mother was not one of these oversharers you hear about in people's pasts, who said too much, or crossed any kind of boundaries between mother and child. I remember a time when my mother explicitly told me, "Your business is your business, but I actually *don't* want to see you kissing your boyfriend." She was extremely good at saying, "I will entertain and answer any factual questions. I will try to talk to you about anything you want to talk about." But she also made it really clear that she thought it was not wise to be having sex at a young age, and that her life was her life and my life was my life.

So I was free to make my own decisions. That was 100 percent clear. In terms of parenting, it was one of the best decisions my mother ever made.

As a woman in today's American society, there's still something in me that makes me feel like my body isn't a great place to live. I didn't get that from my mother. That feeling came from somewhere else—the culture, and maybe feeling rejected by my father, and whatever other possibilities. But I haven't spent a lot of time thinking about it because it wasn't a huge problem for me. It just wasn't.

My initial sexual relationship? We were in love, and we were both virgins, and we had sex. I started young, as much as my mother had expressed her opinion that it wasn't wise to be having sex so young. I was just barely fifteen. I didn't super enjoy sex until later. Maybe I didn't have fabulous orgasms for the first couple years, but all the boyfriends I had in high school were loving, and we had positive sexual experiences.

Because I've always felt free to make my own decisions about sex, I've slept with a lot of people. Because of that fact, I don't even talk about numbers. I learned over time that you have to not tell people how many people you've slept with. Whether you've slept with a lot of people or you haven't slept with that many, people tend to judge you. They're really just using you as a measuring stick to judge themselves.

Certainly I did sleep with people I didn't really want to sleep with. I've definitely had sex I didn't really want to have. But I've never been aggressively made to have sex. I've had no trauma of that sort. Have I been subjected to strong persuasion?—Yeah, kinda. But I've never really truly said no and been ignored.

Then again, I didn't say no very much! I mean, that's the reality of it! I didn't say no, and I did a lot of pursuing. So yeah, I really was a girl who couldn't say no, and by and large I don't regret it.

There was one guy I slept with when I was in the phase of my addiction where I didn't drink, but I was a really heavy marijuana user. This guy— we had the most awesome super-hot flirtation thing going on. Like, it was *so hot.* And the *second* I slept with him, it was just—*over.* Because he was selfish as a lover. He just wanted me to do all the work. So I sort of regret sleeping with him.

That happened on a number of occasions. Cause when you're actively pursuing sex, you end up having a lot of boring sex. I learned that a lot of times the sex isn't worth whatever you might hope to get out of the connection. That's the truth.

This whole double standard is very, very active in most men's brains—the double standard that says women aren't supposed to want sex, and men are. Numerous times I'd go to bed with somebody pretty quickly, or pursued them to have sex, and then they'd tell me, "You must really, really like me, so we can't see each other." They would assume that, to want to have sex with them, I wanted to get my claws into them and have this long commitment.

Either that or they thought that if I wanted so much to have sex with them, then there was something weird about me. As though if a woman has a strong sex drive, then she's definitely strange.

So by the time I got to be about thirty, I often felt like, with whatever guy it was, *Maybe I just won't even bother having sex.*

As much as I made my own choices, I made some pretty bad ones, for real. I had a whole subset of friends toward the end of my non-sobriety who were just utterly baffled by the people I got interested in. For example, at one time I was completely wrapped up in this guy who was a poet. And, um, he was also a drug dealer. It was just a mess. And one of my friends said, "I just thought you would *know,* Olivia—the poets, they're never-go-there types of people!"

Not to mention it's not exactly an awesome decision to get involved with a drug dealer. That relationship, sexually, was quite satisfying, but it was just a disaster emotionally.

I still feel like the most satisfying sex I've had was within relationships of love and care. But those relationships weren't possible when I was out there drinking and using. When I was around thirty, in the years just before I got into recovery, and I wasn't seeing anyone in a relationship anymore, and I was just out there drinking and drugging, the choices I made then were appalling. Just appalling.

I had this period of mainly smoking pot. I was a pothead for sure. I managed to be pretty functional because I had jobs that kept me from being baked all day. I'd have crush after crush after crush, and every single guy was inappropriate. During that period, I'd sleep around, and then I'd feel like, *This is really unsatisfying.*

I preferred to have a really hot make-out session, then go home and masturbate. Cause, like, the *bother* of actually having sex, actually being with another person and his body, was too much.

The minute I got sober, I got into a relationship that was born to fail. Of course my sponsor at the time had told me I shouldn't get into a relationship for a whole year. I told her about this guy and she was just like, "Well—what can you tell any of these women? Not a damn thing!" She was very hands-off. I told her about it, but I wasn't able to be honest about the whole thing with her at that time.

I was about a year clean when I met my husband. I was still seeing the first guy I'd met right after I got sober. So my husband was only the second guy I met while in recovery. Which maybe contributed to the rose-colored glasses.

After I got into recovery I discovered that I'm actually more vanilla than I'd always acted. Maybe it's just about getting older; who knows? My actual physical response has obviously improved, because I'm not numb all the time. Or preoccupied about when my next joint is.

My sex life as a married person is not what I'd like it to be. Honestly, if I had my druthers it would be a little kinkier, but just not in the way that my husband would like it to be kinky. I would just like more experimentation, more variety—positions, and like the kind of stuff you try because you're just playing. My best lovers have been very playful, willing to try stuff and then willing to say, "Well, this ain't gonna happen!" There's something like that missing.

And I think part of it is my husband and I have big communication problems, and maybe I'm not communicating the way I should about this. I also feel my efforts to communicate have been rebuffed due to insecurity.

It's also just a fact that his sexual interests and mine don't really match. He's very porn-y. And I'm not, really. He's more into the idea of role-playing and personas and dressing up, and I'm willing to entertain that as a kind of game, but as a consistent thing I'm just not into role-playing. I don't connect to that at all. It doesn't get me anywhere.

I just want to be two people, getting it on.

There's a weird thing that happens when two people have sex: they sort of feel like they know each other. I love that phrase, "I have *known* this person." Because even if you don't really know anything about someone, there's something you feel like you *know* about them after you've had sex with them.

And I've wondered about that as the spiritual part of sexuality. How? Because there's an essentially spiritual *happening* when you have sex with someone—unless of course it's abusive sex. You share something very fundamental. That metaphor of "knowing" someone—there's something spiritual that I connect to about that.

I haven't written about a "sexual ideal," the way some people say the recovery literature asks us to do. That's one thing I consider to be extremely mired in the patriarchal past of recovery programs. I don't play the patriarchy card very often when I talk about programs, but the "sex ideal" is one time I do.

I think it's a great idea for men. The situation is different for women, but there's no question in my mind that a lot of men need to do that. You gotta know that those old guys who wrote the books, when they were out there, sleeping around on their wives and stuff, they were culpable for lots of shitty behavior perpetrated against women, and they needed to fuckin' face it. They needed to identify their own values and to try to understand that your sexuality is part of your spiritual person.

I've talked to enough young men to realize that they engage in a lot of insane thinking and behavior about sex and women. And when you do damage to someone else through sexuality, that's some serious shit. I think because of patriarchal culture, guys are allowed to live in this delusion that they're not responsible for a lot of stuff they're responsible for. They think it's up to the woman to say yes or no, and beyond that, they're absolved of anything they do.

I wrote a sex *inventory* because I knew that I had damaged a few people along the way with sexual behaviors. And so I wanted to do my Eighth and Ninth Steps about those things. I wanted to make amends. But as a separate kind of "ideal," I'm like, no.

I caution newcomers against sexual entanglements too early. I had to be older and have more time in recovery to see this fundamental spiritual quality to sexuality. And given the fact that we're raised in this sex-negative culture, and so many of us have problems with sex and even with talking about sex, in general I'm inclined to tell a newcomer, "Umm, probably not a good idea right now." Not because I'm shaming her, or because you shouldn't want to have sex, but just to say, "This shit is complicated and it has a way of bringing out bad behavior in everybody."

It's true that I have no fear of sex. And I think that's intimately connected to my upbringing. A lot of women walk around with fear about their sexuality, and it's an absolute fuckin' shame. Nobody should have to feel that way. I mean, a lot of men also feel that way, let's be clear. The culture encourages us to judge our sexual desires and feel bad about them. And we have very few outlets for talking about all this.

I want to say, I don't think you have to have super-spiritual sex to have a good time. And I think it's absolutely okay for people to have sex just to have a good time. But in order to have a good time and *just* have a good time, everybody's gotta be on the same fuckin' page, right? I'm thinking of this one guy I slept with in college on his birthday. It was just like, "Okay, let's have sex!"–you know? He is just a really decent human being. I was into having sex with him. He's a really sexy guy. We had a great time, and we've joked about it since. And it wasn't like a deep emotional experience, but everybody had the time they wanted to have, and there was no bullshit about it. So that is absolutely possible, and I think people should be able to have that kind of sex in their lives without judgment from anywhere.

Sex outside of relationship can be like fast food. It tastes great. It can be exactly what you need at a given moment. Many factors contribute to your desire to eat fast food and your feeling of satiety when you're done.

But living on it? Who wants that?

Having sex is actually one of the last ways we can play as adults. I mean in that kind of non-self-conscious way that children are fully playing, and they don't have judgments, they don't have goals. They're just doing it. I think it's important to have sexual experiences that are like that. They can be had within the context of commitment.

I personally think they're better when they're in the context of relationship. That's sort of the gold standard for me.

GABRIEL

Discovering Unconditional
Love in Community

Sixty-two / Thirty years in recovery

There was this group of men who were my age—mid-thirties—or somewhat older. Remember, this is 1986 through '88 or '89, before protease inhibitors, which changed the whole treatment and made it possible for people to survive a long time.

I'd gotten sober in 1986. I don't know how many of these guys had been tested before they got sober. I think they learned in sobriety. It became one of the things you learned, because when you got clean and sober you began to take care of yourself. And I know of at least ten people who died within that period of about three years.

I grew up in New York City. I started using dope in college, and I started really getting into heroin around 1978, in my mid-twenties.

I was a nice, tucked-in junkie. I could hold it in, and I didn't vomit until I got to a toilet. At least, I didn't until the last couple of years I was using. I could control when I'd throw up and who I'd fight with.

My primary substances were opiates and coke, or speed. I preferred opiates, but I did speed so I'd have a level of energy to work. And I liked speedballing. To me, that was the perfect thing, but I also drank constantly. I flattered myself that I didn't drink to get drunk, although I certainly got wasted.

I got sober in Baltimore. I was thirty-two. I lived in Hampden, near Hopkins. At first I just went to NA in Baltimore. And then I'd go to AA meetings in New York, because I had business that took me there about once a month, and there were meetings there that specifically welcomed people with drug histories.

My home group is Completely Sober in Chelsea. It was one of the first meetings that welcomed discussion of drugs as well as alcohol. It kept losing its space, so over the years the meeting has moved around a lot. It was originally at St. Francis Xavier Church at Fifteenth Street. It moved to the French Church on Sixteenth, then it moved to St. Bernard's Church. Now it meets at a senior center on Nineteenth and Ninth.

It's a meeting with a real history. It got very fabulous in the mid- to late-eighties—it was an extremely glamorous meeting. Lots of young club kids went there—a lot of actors, a lot of musicians. People went there to be seen. When I got sober, it was where I saw people I'd gotten high with. I hadn't necessarily been friends with them, but they were the people who worked at the clubs I went to. For example, there was a guy I knew who'd been a bouncer at Danceteria, and now he's a Vipassana meditation teacher.

At one point, the meeting had to move to a church that was primarily for Mexican immigrants. We'd meet in the basement. It had no floor. You'd walk on the joists. There'd be mice; it was cold—it was awesome. There were maybe fifteen regulars who attended come rain or shine. That was a beautiful, beautiful meeting.

There was a guy named Jimmy. He was a designer. He projected very butch—he had a crew cut and he was ripped, but he was as queer as a three-dollar bill. People were in awe of him, including me, and I'm straight. He sponsored a lot of people. And a lot of people took care of him when he was dying.

That was another thing—the meeting took care of people when they were dying. It was quite beautiful. People would send food. If a guy had to go to a hospital, somebody would go with him. And especially for New York City, that's something. Because a lot of people had been disowned by their families for being gay and out and contracting this disease because of their sexuality. There were a few people who reconciled with their families, and there were a couple people who just went back to their families, to die.

Because that was the thing: nobody was gonna get better.

They would come to meetings and share about their bitterness. It wasn't like they *weren't* bitter. They went *through* their bitterness. Because anybody who learns in their thirties or forties that they're dying—I don't think anybody like that isn't bitter.

Watching them taught me about the Seventh Step and self-acceptance. Up until then I'd thought, *Oh—you just* accept *stuff.* I learned that from being in hard-core old-fashioned AA and NA meetings—by which I mean, they had members who'd say, "You just *accept.* You gotta *accept.*" Their attitude was, acceptance is almost muscular effort: "It's a spiritual program! And if you don't *hit your knees,* you're gonna *pick up!*"

These guys in New York who were dying showed me that acceptance is not just a single act. It's a process. I watched them say, "I'm gonna go through this, and I'm gonna be wretched about it and scream and kick as much as I have to, and then I'll be open to becoming something else."

I learned that you don't *will* the Seventh Step to happen to you. It's something that you come to, that you arrive at. My experience is that I've never just decided, "Oh, I'm gonna get rid of this defect." You become entirely ready to face the shit, and then you enact your readiness by going *through* the shit. And I would say that *that's* the process of acceptance.

These young people, these young men who had been healthy and beautiful, and had gloried in the sexual and sensual pleasure their bodies could give them, had discovered that they were sick in the most horrendous, humiliating ways. Watching sores break out on their skin. Losing bowel control. Of course they were bitter about it, and terrified. And then at a certain point, they gave up their bitterness and came to accept it: "This is what's gonna happen to me."

They brought all these experiences to the home group.

When they were very sick, we'd take meetings to their homes, or to their hospital rooms. It was beautiful. It was wonderful. Those were times when I felt like, "*This* is what recovery is—you form a community, and you bring people what they need."

The thing is, I've done plenty of Twelfth-Step calls. But to be totally honest, I don't love the people I make those calls for. In theory I do, but I'm doing it for me. I'm doing it because it's the service you give in order to stay sober. But to be really brutally honest, I don't care about them. Which is to say, I don't have an emotional cathexis with the people I've brought Twelfth-Step calls to.

But back then, in that meeting, I was caring for people I knew and I'd gotten sober with, who I'd known for three or four years and looked up to. Jimmy probably had ten years more than I did in recovery. If he had lived, he'd have forty years. He'd be very old now—he'd be about seventy.

I often feel like having so much time in recovery simply means I have more years of being less attached to anything, but that's also Buddhism—I mean, it's years of sitting in meditation. And sometimes I think it's just being old! Now that I'm getting older, and I have a lot of recovery time, I can see that I don't really want much of anything. I don't want riotous sex as much as I want a decent night's sleep! If I fall asleep and I sleep through the night, I'm ecstatic.

Those guys taught me more than anyone else has about how you work a program. Being a part of that home group formed me as a person. They formed the way I looked at sexuality and at partners. And also they taught me about true sobriety. Because one of the illusions in sobriety is that you get sober and everything changes—the shorthand for it that I heard at Completely Sober is "Cash and Prizes." The illusion is, you get sober and the cash and prizes roll in. I don't much like it when meetings emphasize the Ninth Step promises, but the important one to me is that "we will intuitively know how to handle situations that used to baffle us." Because that's true. It's just another way of saying we learn to accept ourselves.

Those guys knew how it was gonna end up. They had to face the truth. It was the kind of dire situation that a lot of people would use as an excuse to get loaded. And they didn't. And that was very beautiful. In a way it became a capstone of their sobriety.

The experience of being with those recovering men who were dying taught me how to truly be part of a fellowship. As an example—I have a friend at my home group who committed suicide last year, and I stopped everything to go and be with her husband and attend the memorial.

That experience also taught me to trust in a power greater than myself. Or a power other than myself. I'd say that the Third, Sixth, and Seventh Steps have taught me the most about delivering myself over to the care of something else. And what is this care? I learned that, well, it's not necessarily that you're gonna be kept healthy, and happy, and safe.

So what is it? What is the guarantee?

It's a very mysterious thing. Speaking of it practically, I'd say the guarantee is that if I take these Steps, I'm *never* gonna have to get loaded again. I might not be healthy, happy, or safe, but I will be *awake* in my life. And I won't be the agent of my own betrayal anymore.

Afterword

· · · · · · · · · · · · · · ·

As we have seen, distortion of the truth is one of the central features of addiction. This distortion is by no means an individualistic problem—it's systemic. We live in an addictive society that promulgates distorted images of human sexuality: as seduction, humiliation, superficiality, and pain, conflating all these with titillation. We're afraid of real eroticism because it requires surrender. If we take steps to move back into our bodies and to connect not with the pornographic but with the erotic—and there's a difference—the culture warns us that chaos, hedonism, and bacchanalia will ensue. And if we put our trust in these cultural forces, there goes our sobriety, because we don't trust ourselves with our own bodies.

In so many ways, we're encouraged to disconnect. We crave human touch, but we resist engaging in it. We don't want to look at either the suffering or the real possibility of deep, life-giving human connection. We'd rather surf Tinder or Twitter, or binge on Netflix or pizza. We reach for our phones.

But in reality, our bodies—our incarnation as embodied, whole, sane, erotic beings—are what will truly bring us a living, dynamic recovery from addiction.

In the face of this widespread distortion and denial, recovery communities are a countercultural force for healing and compassion. We tell our stories. We listen to others' stories. We build supportive communities. We ask for help. For an hour, we shut our phones off. And we don't use. It's what we do.

In what other places outside of our recovery communities can we do these things? How early in life can we start—for example, by helping our kids shut their off their devices, by asking them to tell the stories of their days, by looking each other in the eyes?

Meditation, yoga, prayer—these are the stalwart practices of the Eleventh Step that help foster mental stillness and self-acceptance. These practices are vital because they help us experience the passing of feelings. As important as that is, we also need to communicate with others. That includes practicing community within the circles of our families and friends, not just in recovery groups. And that practice can help transform our culture, too. Honesty about sex in recovery can pave the way for a broader honesty in our culture. As we discern the differences and commonalities between sex and intimacy, we can make choices about our behaviors and relationships with more awareness. And as we begin to talk more openly about sex, we can serve as examples for others that it is possible to find their own sexual memories, desires, needs, and voices. Those of us in recovery have a chance to be cultural leaders by insisting that our society move toward honesty and forthrightness about sexuality. **To that extent, recovery is for everyone.**

Whether we've been through trauma or not, speaking our stories out loud is the critical first step: we're taking action that can move us toward sexual intimacy and understanding, first with ourselves and then with others. Telling our stories helps us acknowledge our experiences and perceptions of events. It counteracts the persistent tendency to distort the truth. It can motivate us to get help in reconnecting with our bodies. Telling our stories helps us form the community that supports our inbuilt capacity for resilience—finding a power greater than ourselves that has actually resided inside ourselves all along.

Besides telling our stories, it's also vital to practice Eleventh Step suggestions, and it can help to do that in groups. Meditation, yoga, prayer, and other forms of physical and mental stillness and self-acceptance all help us experience the passing of feelings. Rather than "agents of our own betrayal," as Gabriel so poignantly put it, we can become our own greatest allies. The people who speak in this book prove that possibility for all of us.

• • •

Acknowledgments

I'm fortunate to be loved by a spectacular throng of friends and family. I'm grateful that they put up with my losing major parts of my mind when I'm up to my neck in pages, and that they always show interest in the questions I'm asking and the stories I'm telling. Thank you for actually answering when you see my name appear on your screens: Judy, Von, Kathy, Lori, Laurel, Emily, Mary Jo, Pat, Deborah, Kathie, Moira, Suz, Nancy, the two beautiful Jims, and the one and only Daniel. And above all, thanks to my son, Jonathan, for believing in me and my work, and for speaking with me in so many voices.

For teaching me how to help others without completely draining the well, thanks to my anonymous young'uns, who always seem to call at the right time.

For candid and free-ranging interviews that took place between May 2015 and January 2016, sincere thanks to Rosalyn Dischiavo, Sarah Hepola, Nina Jablonski, Emily Nagoski, Tiffany Field, and Greg Siegle. Your thoughtful perspectives helped shape my ideas about the intertwining of sexuality and substance abuse, and you gave me tools with which to listen (many times) to those whose stories I've told and to those whose stories are not told here but instead form the deep, rich background for *Sex in Recovery*.

For guidance, I thank Dr. Michael Genovese, Patty Powers, Chloe Mills, Renee Jennings, Ruwan Meepagala, Jen Lemen, Lisa Jacobs, Tracey Cleantis, and at Hazelden, Vanessa Torrado, a true writer's editor, Mindy Keskinen for her copyediting, the skilled and indefatigable Emily Reller, and my editor, Sid Farrar. I especially would like to thank Kris Knieriem and Steve Lowry of Blender, Inc. in Pittsburgh for helping this book be tall.

Most of all, I'm grateful to the remarkable people who consented to speak their stories out loud for us. I wish I could thank you all by name. I'm so happy and humbled to know you as well as I do. May your stories help others to be known as well.

Notes

1. Alcoholics Anonymous, *Alcoholics Anonymous,* 4th ed. (New York: Alcoholics Anonymous World Services, 2000).

2. "A Word about Quaker Queries." Friends General Conference, at www .fgcquaker.org/sites/www.fgcquaker.org/files/attachments/A%20Word%20 about%20Quaker%20Queries_1.pdf. Accessed June 11, 2016.

3. Ming-Chyi Huang et al., "Impact of Multiple Types of Childhood Trauma Exposure on Risk of Psychiatric Comorbidity Among Alcoholic Inpatients," *Alcoholism: Clinical and Experimental Research* 36, no. 6 (2012): 1099–1107.

4. Stephanie Covington and Janet Kohen, "Women, Alcohol, and Sexuality," *Advances in Alcohol and Substance Abuse* 4, no. 1 (Fall 1984), 41–56.

5. Shanta R. Dube et al., "Childhood Abuse, Neglect, and Household Dysfunction and the Risk of Illicit Drug Use: The Adverse Childhood Experiences Study," *Pediatrics* Vol. 111, No. 3 (2003), 564–572.

6. Emily Nagoski, *Come as You Are: The Surprising New Science That Will Transform Your Sex Life* (New York: Simon & Schuster, 2015), Kindle AZW file.

7. Patrick Carnes with Joseph M. Moriarity, *Sexual Anorexia: Overcoming Sexual Self-Hatred* (Center City, MN: Hazelden, 1997), 52–53.

8. Sarah Hepola, "The Alcohol Blackout," *Texas Monthly,* January 2016, accessed at www.texasmonthly.com/the-culture/the-alcohol-blackout/.

9. Nina Jablonski, *Skin: A Natural History* (Berkeley: University of California Press, 2003), Kindle AZW file.

10. One reason some drugs cause a warm glow to blossom in our bellies is that there are many receptors for particular neurotransmitters in the gastrointestinal (GI) system. Science writer Adam Hadhazy put it this way: "The enteric nervous system uses more than 30 neurotransmitters, just like the brain, and in fact 95 percent of the body's serotonin is found in the bowels. Because antidepressant medications called selective serotonin reuptake

inhibitors (SSRIs) increase serotonin levels, it's little wonder that meds meant to cause chemical changes in the mind often provoke GI issues as a side effect" (Hadhazy, in "Think Twice: How the Gut's 'Second Brain' Influences Mood and Well-Being," *Scientific American*, February 12, 2010, accessed at www.scientificamerican.com/article/gut-second-brain/). The same happens with painkillers, because the GI tract is rich with opioid receptors. And kissing activates the reward neurotransmitter dopamine, half of which is made in the gut.

There's also good reason to think that the heart also has its own brain. In the words of one neuroscientist, "Besides releasing hormones, regulating blood pressure, and influencing the body's magnetic field, the 'small brain' in the heart can thus act on the emotional brain via these direct nerve connections. And when the heart loses its balance, the emotional brain is immediately affected." Meditation restores this balance (David Servan-Schreiber, *The Instinct to Heal: Curing Depression, Anxiety and Stress Without Drugs and Without Talk Therapy.* Emmaus, PA: Rodale Press, 2003, 40).

11. Kissing, and all of human sexuality, is about "capital-T Truth . . . about life *before* death." David Foster Wallace, "This Is Water," 2005, accessed at http://bulletin.kenyon.edu/x4280.html.

12. "The Turtle and the Hare" aired August 2, 1998 and made the Vibratex Rabbit Pearl one of the bestselling vibrators of all time.

13. "Transcripts of Journey to Recovery with Joe M. and Charlie P.," accessed at www.164fl.com/Joe_and_Charlie.pdf, p. 125.

14. Emily Nagoski, "Pleasure Is the Measure: One Simple Rule to Radically Improve Your Sex Life," *The Dirty Normal*, August 4, 2015, accessed at www.thedirtynormal.com/blog/2015/08/04/one-simple-rule-to-radically-improve-your-sex-life/.

15. Nagoski, *Come as You Are*, Chapter 2.

16. Esther Perel, "The Secret to Desire in a Long-Term Relationship," *TED Talk*, February 14, 2013, www.youtube.com/watch?v=sa0RUmGTCYY.

17. John M. Gottman, *The Science of Trust: Emotional Attunement for Couples* (New York: W. W. Norton, 2011), 130.

18. Writers I'm thinking of include Melody Beattie, Claudia Black, John Bradshaw, and Charlotte Kasl. There are many others.

19. David Fawcett, "After Meth: A Gay Man's Guide to Sex and Recovery, Part 2: Tools for Change," Presentation at Bureau of General Services Queer

Division LBGTQ Center, New York City, Dec. 13, 2015, www.youtube.com/watch?v=3w7PLi2gGk0.

20. Julie E. Cohen, "What Privacy Is For," *Harvard Law Review,* May 20, 2013, accessed at http://harvardlawreview.org/2013/05/what-privacy-is-for/.

21. Donald R. Taylor, MD, "The Pharmacology of Fentanyl and Its Impact on Pain Management: Lipid Solubility," *Medscape Multispecialty,* accessed online at www.medscape.org/viewarticle/518441_2. On the other hand, when you take fentanyl or any fat-soluble drug long-term, it saturates your body's fat cells. And stored this way, they can become poisonous. Think of the difference between water-soluble Vitamin C and fat-soluble Vitamins A, D, E, and K. If you take too much Vitamin C, the body will simply pee it out. But long-term exposure to fat-soluble vitamins leads to their accumulation in fat cells, especially in the liver, where they continue to exert effects on the body.

Once the body begins to filter out—detoxify—chemicals stored in fat cells, the liver converts them into water-soluble chemicals that are then released into the blood. Which is partly why, when we're detoxing from long-term exposure to fat-soluble drugs such as fentanyl, methadone, and benzodiazepines such as Xanax and Ativan, we feel so crappy for so long. This state is called "post-acute withdrawal syndrome," and unfortunately, people who aren't prepared for it may get impatient. Many are driven back to using because they think the pain of the process will never end.

22. Alana Massey, "Against Chill," *Medium,* https://medium.com/matter/against-chill-930dfb60a577#.4nprwfpnx.

23. So many factors play into women's difficulty with orgasm. Some women can never orgasm under any circumstance; some can orgasm only with penetration; some can orgasm with penetration with added clitoral stimulation, but not reliably; some can frequently orgasm with penetration and clitoral stimulation; and some can easily orgasm with just penetration, or even with just nipple stimulation. I have read over and over that some women who have "mind" orgasms by just thinking their way there. I believe it, but still, *hmmm.*

Our ideas of what's "normal" are shaped by both scientific and anecdotal evidence—sometimes by scholarly studies but overwhelmingly by popular reports that we read while standing in line at the grocery store. As one example: "The latest data from the Kinsey Institute indicates that 20 to 30 percent of women don't have orgasms during intercourse. But the number is likely much higher, says Carol Queen, staff sexologist and researcher at Good Vibrations, a feminist adult toy shop and education center in San

Francisco. 'The statistic my colleagues and I have been citing lately is that roughly 70 percent of women rarely or never have orgasms with intercourse. That makes it the norm,' she says. 'I think most people have *no idea* so many women have this problem.' Though this number does not come from a scientific study, she says there's a general consensus among her peers in the sexual health community about how high it is." (Heather Wood Rudolph, "The Orgasm Deficit," *Cosmopolitan*, July 8, 2014, www.cosmopolitan.com/sex-love/news/a28359/orgasm-deficit/.) On the one hand, none of Queen's "rough" figures can be scientifically validated. On the other hand, by all accounts, women are discouraged from masturbating and can reach the age of twenty without ever having explored their own bodies, and they regularly fake orgasms because they know no other way—except drinking and drugging, of course—to deal with the stress of *needing* to come, not just for their own pleasure but to prove to the dude that they can—and that the dude can *make* them come.

24. Facilitated by New York City–based sober coach Patty Powers and held every first Sunday of the month on www.intherooms.com.

25. With respect to the most awesome sex advice columnist Dan Savage, who coined the term "GGG" (good, giving, and game).

About the Author

Jennifer Matesa is author of four nonfiction books about body, mind, and human well-being, including the recently released *The Recovering Body: Physical and Spiritual Fitness for Living Clean and Sober*, also from Hazelden Publishing. She speaks and writes widely, and she teaches English at the University of Pittsburgh. Her long-running site about addiction and recovery, *Guinevere Gets Sober* (http://guineveregetssober. com), was one of the first blogs of its kind and is dedicated to giving the public reliable information without advertising or fees. Her commitment to removing the stigma from addiction and recovery earned her a fellowship at the Substance Abuse and Mental Health Services Administration (SAMHSA).

About Hazelden Publishing

As part of the Hazelden Betty Ford Foundation, Hazelden Publishing offers both cutting-edge educational resources and inspirational books. Our print and digital works help guide individuals in treatment and recovery, and their loved ones. Professionals who work to prevent and treat addiction also turn to Hazelden Publishing for evidence-based curricula, digital content solutions, and videos for use in schools, treatment programs, correctional programs, and electronic health records systems. We also offer training for implementation of our curricula.

Through published and digital works, Hazelden Publishing extends the reach of healing and hope to individuals, families, and communities affected by addiction and related issues.

For more information about Hazelden publications,
please call **800-328-9000**
or visit us online at **hazelden.org/bookstore.**

Also of Interest

The Recovering Body
Physical and Spiritual Fitness for Living Clean and Sober
JENNIFER MATESA

Just as recovery requires daily practice, so do physical fitness and a healthy life-style. In *The Recovering Body*, Jennifer Matesa ignites the recovery community with the first-ever guide to achieving physical recovery as part of the path to life-long sobriety. Combining solid science and practical guidance, along with her own experience and that of other addicts, Matesa frames physical fitness as a living amends to self—a transformative gift analogous to the "spiritual fitness" practices worked on in recovery.
Order No. 7568; ebook EB7568

Girlfriend of Bill
What You Need to Know If You're Dating Someone in Recovery
KAREN NAGY

When Karen Nagy started dating a recovering alcoholic, she sometimes felt she was seeing someone from another planet—a man with his own language, culture, and social behaviors. In this book, she offers a field guide to the Twelve Step way of life, with humor, compassion, and great respect for what it takes to recover from an addiction. Nagy also helps readers to stay alert to—and address—their own possible codependent tendencies, building the potential for a healthy relationship.
Order No. 7536; ebook EB7536

For more information about Hazelden publications,
please call **800-328-9000**
or visit us online at **hazelden.org/bookstore.**